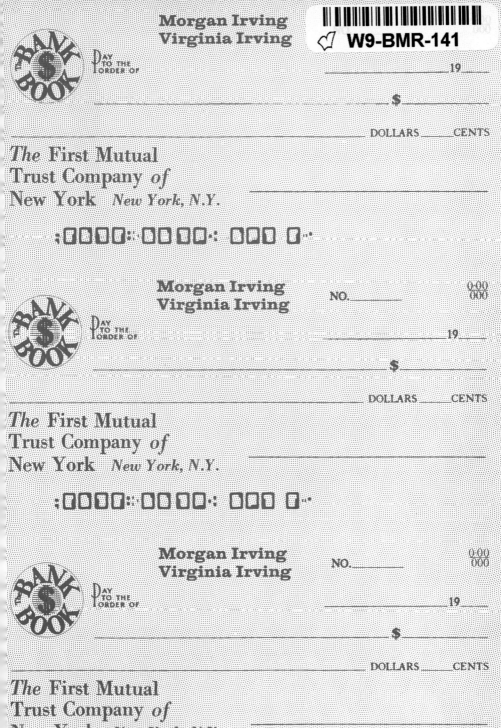

**Morgan Irving**
**Virginia Irving**

W9-BMR-141

PAY TO THE ORDER OF

19____

$____

DOLLARS_____CENTS

*The* First Mutual
Trust Company *of*
New York  *New York, N.Y.*

**Morgan Irving**
**Virginia Irving**

NO.____

0-00
000

PAY TO THE ORDER OF

19____

$____

DOLLARS_____CENTS

*The* First Mutual
Trust Company *of*
New York  *New York, N.Y.*

**Morgan Irving**
**Virginia Irving**

NO.____

0-00
000

PAY TO THE ORDER OF

19____

$____

DOLLARS_____CENTS

*The* First Mutual
Trust Company *of*
New York  *New York, N.Y.*

## BOOKS BY CHARLES SOPKIN

MONEY TALKS!

SEVEN GLORIOUS DAYS, SEVEN FUN-FILLED NIGHTS

FROM THOSE WONDERFUL FOLKS WHO
GAVE YOU PEARL HARBOR
(with Jerry Della Femina)

THE BANK BOOK
(with Morgan Irving)

# THE
# BANK BOOK

# THE
# BANK BOOK

by

## MORGAN IRVING

as audited by

## CHARLES SOPKIN

LITTLE, BROWN AND COMPANY · BOSTON · TORONTO

Library of Congress Cataloging in Publication Data

Irving, Morgan.
  The bank book.

  1.  Banks and banking--United States.    I.  Title.
HG2481.I84              332.1'0973          73-9981
ISBN 0-316-432377

*Published simultaneously in Canada*
*by Little, Brown & Company (Canada) Limited*

PRINTED IN THE UNITED STATES OF AMERICA

*Richard Kluger gave me the idea; Burton M. Fine, Esq., and Sterling Lord made the book possible; Eliot Fremont-Smith offered the initial commitment; and then Louie Howland provided the final assistance. My grateful thanks to all of them.*

# THE
# BANK BOOK

# INTRODUCTION

As I rode to work on March 23, 1973, I browsed through my copy of the *New York Times* and read, in no particular order, the following: the lead story on page one described how the Continental Illinois National Bank and Trust Company of Chicago had cut its prime rate from 6¾ percent to 6½ percent less than a week after a handful of banks had raised their prime rates from 6¼ percent to 6¾ percent. The prime rate is not the rate at which you and I can borrow money from our friendly bank; it is the rate at which very big companies can borrow funds. What had happened to Continental Illinois was that Dr. Arthur F. Burns, the chairman of the Federal Reserve Board, jumped down its throat after it had raised its prime rate. Dr. Burns says he is trying to control inflation for Mr. Nixon, and in his opinion when the seven large banks raised their prime rate, they weren't doing their best to control inflation. Most of my fellow commuters from New Jersey heading into New York City don't understand the prime rate, and I'm sure did not understand why the *Times* led its front page with it.

The second story, also on page one, was probably read by most of the *Times*'s readers that Friday. A supervisor of tellers at a branch of the Union Dime Savings Bank was ar-

rested and charged with the embezzlement of about $1,-
500,000 from his bank. His name was Roswell Steffen, and
he lived in Parlin, New Jersey, and he was a bettor. To the
tune of about $30,000 a day. He had been working at the
bank for nine years and was regarded by his fellow employees as a "real nice fellow." According to the cops, Roswell
had had his hands (and, I guess, his feet) in the till for more
than three years. He'd worked out a system for using the
bank's computer to shift money from account to account.
Aside from the usual quotes from various banking officials
exclaiming at the size of the job, what fascinated me — as
a banker — was that the bank hadn't caught up with Roswell. And if you read between the lines of the *Times,*
Union Dime never would have caught up with Roswell had
not the New York cops had a hand in the proceedings. It
seems that several weeks prior to Roswell's arrest, a huge
bookmaking operation was busted. As the police were sift-
ing through the records of bets placed with the ring, they
came across Roswell's name; it appeared that he'd been laying stupendous amounts each night on basketball games
and horse races. And when they learned, eventually, that he
worked in a bank, the cops took one look at each other and
said that perhaps they ought to keep a close eye on Steffen.
As soon as Union Dime heard of their plunging teller, they
sent in clouds of auditors, and after working around the
clock learned the extent of their disaster. Roswell Steffen
pleaded not guilty and was held on $20,000 bail.

As I worked my way toward the business section of the
paper I came across a small story about a man named Sid-
ney Zneimer whom the Feds were after for evading (so they
said) some $278,000 in taxes. Sidney used to be a vice
president and loan officer of the Royal National Bank of

New York and he had approved a group of loans totaling $75 million to a bunch of the *ragazzi* down in Virginia, names of Charles J. Piluso, Louis Pomponio, Paul Pomponio and Louis Pomponio, Jr. The government is saying that Piluso had given Sidney all that cash for being a swell guy when it came to approving a loan — the cash plus two new cars plus $17,000 worth of decorations for his apartment.

There was a short United Press International story out of Washington in the business pages, which stated that the American Banking Association urged Congress to kill a bill that would force banks to pay interest on personal checking accounts. A spokesman for that grand organization said, "I'd love it if I could collect interest on my checking account, but I'm not sure it's the best thing in the long run." Not much news there.

And finally, the *Times*'s financial columnist, Robert Metz, had a column about the pollster Louis Harris, who took a survey about people's attitudes toward the heads of financial institutions. Brokerage executives had the confidence of only 16 percent of the people surveyed, and finance company executives rated 8 percent in the confidence poll. On the positive side, banks enjoyed an "astoundingly high" rating of 59 percent. Harris said the people were "highly pleased" with the growth of retail services.

I will grant that my industry of banking seemed to have particularly heavy coverage on the day in question. You just don't nab a million-dollar embezzler that often. Nor does the murky prime rate, which confuses everyone including bankers, make the front page every day. But banks do interest people, and it is this interest which has provided the motivation for this book. Essentially, I would like to satisfy people's interest in banks.

A word about the cowardice of the anonymous by-line. In recent years, certain writers have written about various institutions using a variety of names. One of the first books was about the rigors of the internship of a young man in a metropolitan hospital. It was called *Intern* and the author called himself Dr. X. Since *Intern,* revelatory books have come along with authors named "Adam Smith" (*The Money Game* and *Supermoney*), a recent inquiry into the vagaries of the Internal Revenue Service by an Internal Revenue agent who called himself "Diogenes," an amusing but frightening diary by a stockbroker calling himself "Brutus." The name I liked best of all was "Paul Revere," used by a dentist on a book about dentists.

In all of these cases the motivating need for anonymity is quite apparent. My motivation is neither modesty nor coyness; rather, it is outright fear. The banking industry is very much a secret society, and it has a tendency to punish severely those who talk in public about the most innocuous of financial matters.

The name "Morgan Irving" is simply a creation, and it has no relation whatsoever to either Clifford Irving, or Morgan Guaranty, or even Irving Trust. In fact, when the named was created, Irving Trust was running an overwhelmingly ethnic campaign with the selling line, "Call us Irving." That approach has since been wisely dropped.

Even though I hope the reader will accept my need for anonymity and will also accept as fact everything that he reads, the reader does deserve to know something about me, my background, and how this book came to be written.

First of all, I had all the wrong credentials for a banker. I was born into an ordinary family, which happened to be high Episcopalian. Religion, sadly, still has much to do with the structure of banking in New York, and even more sadly, nothing ranks quite as low down the list in a bank as a lower-middle-class Episcopalian. (Well-to-do Episcopalians — ah, that's another story, but unfortunately not my story.) I would say that even the Jews are a bit better off than poor WASPs, and the Irish Catholics probably are a step up from the Jews.

I came from a family of schoolteachers, and they have little status in the banking society. I was born in New Jersey. My parents are alive today, retired, living in a small town in New Jersey, and I live with my wife and two children in northern New Jersey. To be more specific, I fear, is not too sensible.

Although we were not rich, we were devoted to education, and I worked my way through a fair to middling private college in the East and then went on to a poorly rated graduate school of business. If you were to chart the prerequisites for success, I had none of them.

After graduate school I was immediately hauled into the army for my war, the Korean conflict, and through a clerical fluke spent two years in Germany. I wandered about Europe after my discharge and then landed in England and found a job at the British division of First Mutual Trust Company. I spent three years abroad, came back to this country, and have been with the First Mutual Trust ever since. First Mutual Trust, incidentally, is also a creation. The "First" does not relate to First National City Bank, the "Mutual" does not refer to any number of savings and loan institutions, and the "Trust" does not have anything to do with Morgan Guaranty Trust. In short, a madeup name and a play on words.

My career in New York has been one of slow but steady rise, and I now have the title of vice president. A vice president in a bank can mean any grade of assistant vice president, various grades of ordinary vice president, and still further delineations of first vice presidents, senior vice presidents, executive vice presidents. I am in the middle rank, and it is from this point of view that the book is written. Undoubtedly, if I were an anonymous chairman of the board, the book would be pitched on a much different level, and would and should be full of magnificent transactions, skulduggery on an international level.

What I have tried to do in this book is to present those subjects in which I am interested and which will have the most impact on the reader. After all, practically the entire nation at some time or another has used the facilities of a bank, but I don't think that many people really want to know how checks are routed through the New York Clearing House, to take one arcane example. Thus the book contains completely arbitrary contents of what I think I would like to read about a bank if I were not working in a bank. Much of the material is going to bore the banker. He knows about loan policies, how a customer gets or doesn't get a loan. Most bankers avoid talking about bank robberies because most bank robberies are so stupid. This book opens with bank robberies.

Originally there was a complete chapter on the prime rate, but I dropped it because over the course of the three years this book has been in the making the prime rate has gone up, down, sideways, floated, and in yesterday's paper there was some strange talk about having two prime rates: one for the good customers, the other for the not-so-good. Very few people at our bank understand the prime rate, and I finally threw the chapter out.

There are ways to beat the banks, but my Episcopalian upbringing reared its righteous head, and thus the reader looking for tips on how to forge checks, kite checks, embezzle money, rob banks, will not find solace here. God is watching us always, especially in the postdating of checks.

I have attempted to bring some color to a deliberately bland and colorless institution. Bankers cringe at one of their number deviating from what they regard as normal behavior. I find it amusing that one of the officers at our bank spends his entire lunch hour at the Doubleday book store on Fifth Avenue and Fifty-third Street in New York. The store has a modern, twisting staircase and the officer, Landis Geiger, walks over to the store every day, positions himself near the staircase, idly thumbs through a book, and looks up the dresses of the nubile young women going from the first floor to the second. There is quite a lot of material in this book on bank officers, how they are initiated into the priesthood, how they fall from grace.

I have devoted an entire chapter to the madness of bank credit cards, and since we are a people devoted to paper money, I thought the space was worth it. For those of us living in New York, who watch entire blocks demolished at the whim of a builder, keeping your eye on your bank can sometimes be a frustrating sport. Therefore, I have a chapter on bank location and its rationale.

Influence is a watchword of banks and it eventually affects all of us. Within the bounds of decency and taste, and aware of the laws of libel, I have tried to present some illustrative cases of how influence in a bank works.

Decency and taste present a problem at times in writing about banks, because some of the people in banks are neither decent nor tasteful. The masking of identification regarding individuals has been total, I assure you, to protect everyone concerned. First Mutual Trust is one of the largest banks in the United States, but I don't think that anyone either in or out of the banking field will be able to identify the bank positively.

My only true regret is that I have to continue working at First Mutual Trust for a living. If I didn't, the stories would be more bizarre than they are. The whole truth about banking from any level is a fascinating blend of greed, ignorance, prejudice, and complete indifference to the public good. How we present ourselves to the public is, obviously, a different story.

But I have not presented anecdotes or stories just for the sake of idle entertainment. One of the most intriguing officers in all of New York banking is a latent jet pilot named Ed Gutwillig. He operates a huge region up in Westchester County, but lives for flying his private plane. Every day he phones the bank to let them know he's on the job, but as soon as the lunch hour approaches he races to his plane, and spends two hours aloft. His expense account is larded appropriately to pay for the aviation fuel. Unfortunately, I could not see my way clear to making any significance or sense out of Gutwillig, so he will have to remain content with this brief mention and be happy with the knowledge that he is the only bank officer I know who has read *Jonathan Livingston Seagull* eight times.

# CHAPTER I

THAT story just about sums up bank robbers. Willie Sut-
ton to the contrary, most bank robbers are stupid,
and generally they are failures at their chosen profession.
Bankers, in turn, bore easily at the mention of bank robbers. Ask a banker for some thrilling bank robbery stories,
and he'll promptly tell you that Penn Central going down
the tubes in 1970 may well turn out to be the greatest bank
robbery story of all time, followed only in quality by the
near-collapse of Lockheed. Then, of course, there is Lam-
mot du Pont Copeland III, known affectionately to his

friends as Motsie, who went into personal bankruptcy to the tune of $27 million, taking a couple of banks, a toy company, a women's college, and assorted ventures and debentures along with him. Motsie, however, is strictly small potatoes and really not in the same league with Lockheed and Penn Central.

But still my nonbanking friends keep asking me to tell them about bank robberies. I am planning to introduce this rather personal look at banking with a selection of bank heists, all true, a few sad, but most a monument to man's stupidity toward his fellow man.

At First Mutual Trust Company of New York, we have a policy of rewarding the tellers who happen to be at the receiving end of a bank robbery. Depending on the severity of the situation (i.e., gunfire or not, wounded citizenry or not) we give our tellers (most of whom are women) a dozen roses for having survived the robbery. If, in the line of duty, the teller screams and faints on the spot, as some tellers have done, she gets a day off plus the roses. I remember some discussion in our executive dining room a few years ago about the cost of roses — there had been a frost somewhere and the price of roses had gone up — and one of the senior vice presidents said simply that First Mutual Trust would not tolerate a substitute for roses. So roses it has remained.

The real problem with bank robberies, and where the potential for danger lies, is that usually all parties concerned are astonishingly dumb: robber, teller, bank guard. This can make for a dangerous situation which may result in violence. We do not like violence when they rob First Mutual: let them take the money and get the hell out of the branch so we can go about our business. Violence means embarrassing visits from insurance companies, unpleasant telephone calls from the press, and loads of cops looking for robbers. No sir, no violence.

A recent robbery to illustrate the point. We have a branch out in Brooklyn on a busy downtown street which must have six other competitive bank branches along the same block.

One day last fall, a branch manager happened to take a look outside the window and noticed a suspicious car cruising up and down the street, very slowly, back and forth. You do begin to get a sixth sense about these things, and the manager, very wisely, took down the license plate of the car and forgot about it.

A couple of days later the same car appeared on the block, and since the license plate number had been distributed to all of the managers on the block, someone spotted the car immediately and called the police. In the car were two budding robbers, each with an enormous bandana tied across his face. I can assure you that there are more effective disguises; Sundance Kid—style handkerchiefs are a bit passé. So there are our two robbers sitting in their car, and they're terribly nervous. One of them is so nervous, in fact, that he has to go to the bathroom. He spots a bar across the street, tells his partner to hold it a minute, and gets out of the car, walks across a busy Brooklyn street and enters the bar. It is a tribute to the patrons of this particular bar that not one soul looked up when the thief walked into the bar, bandana still in place, asked the bartender where the bathroom was, got a nonchalant nod toward the rear of the bar, walked the entire length of the bar without raising an eyebrow, went about his business, walked out of the bar and back across the street, and climbed into the car where his partner was getting increasingly nervous.

You may draw any conclusions you wish from this little vignette of city life in New York; my feeling about it is simply that today we live in an age of total costume, and a man walking about the streets in a bandana is almost typically dressed. At any rate, the two robbers got out of their car, pulled out revolvers, and walked into a bank, announcing in a slight obligato, "This is a holdup."

Because there have been so many bank robberies in New York City recently, the customers froze automatically in tableau. What follows is absolutely true because it happened in a bank managed by a close friend of mine. The robber went up to one of the tellers' windows, repeated that this was, in the jargon, a "stickup," and demanded her money. Her answer was the classic bank teller snarl: "My window is shut. You gotta go to another window." This response from a teller is so indelibly ingrained in the minds of the entire banking public that the robbers reacted not like robbers but like customers: they cursed briefly and walked to another cage. At the second cage the teller simply said she didn't have any money; by the time the robbers got to the third window they were getting quite nervous. The manager, who was observing the entire charade from the platform, was practically hysterical. "For God's sake," he screamed, "will someone give them some money." Finally, one of the tellers heaved a sack of money over the window; the robbers, by this time bordering on hysteria themselves, grabbed it and ran out the front door. Waiting at the door, naturally, were about ninety police who promptly grabbed the robbers and the sack containing $34. If it hadn't been for the fact that the robbers had guns, the incident would almost have fallen into the petit larceny category.

To illustrate the problem with robberies: it is very difficult if not impossible to successfully rob a bank because banks, although foolish in many areas of operation, are quite bright when it comes to protecting themselves. Tellers are paid $115 a week; if they survive twenty years with our bank they might get up to $140 a week. In today's labor market, $115 a week does not buy you much in the way of either ambition or intelligence. (That $115 a week is an average; tellers start at $95 a week and then work *up* to $115 a week.) Yet the key to modern banking is the teller. My bank, like every large New York bank and every large bank throughout the country, relies on its retail business through its branches to survive. Although most large banks have a national banking division and an international banking division, the emphasis in U.S. banking today is being placed on retail banking, a most lucrative field.

If you take the three components of a typical robbery — bank guard, bank teller, and robber — you'll see that all three categories are on the bottom economic rung. If the teller is underpaid, and I assure you all of them are, then the bank guard is even more underpaid. (If you owned a business and needed a cashier, someone you could trust, because anywhere between $5,000 and $10,000 a day or even more might pass through her hands, would you hire her at $95 a week and after twenty years perhaps pay her $140 a week?)

With regard to the bank guards, what can one say? They, too, are hired at $95 a week. If they attend what we laughingly call "Gun School," at which they're taught how to use a gun and told never to use it, they get an additional $10 a week, which brings them up to $105 a week. And no more. Never a raise. They're not clever people, and coupled with this is a singular lack of ambition; many of them are retired cops or firemen. They're very happy ambling around the branch, straightening out deposit slips, getting people to stay in line, answering questions that they're able to. Bank guards think that their job is one of prestige; tellers don't even have the vestiges of prestige to cling to.

The teller at $115 a week, the guard at $105 a week, and the robber himself — usually a junkie. As I have said, they are a terribly volatile mix. It amazes me that more people aren't injured during robberies.

At First Mutual Trust Company we have about three attempted robberies a week, which is neither high nor low as an industry average. We've got 126 branches. (At least the last time I looked we had 126 branches. One of our branches was built on top of an old garbage dump and it has been quietly sinking into the landfill a foot or so a year. For all I know it's up to its vault in garbage now, so the number of branches might well be 125.)

You don't read that we're robbed 140 times a year; bank robbery stories only get into the papers when the circumstances surrounding them are unusual: i.e., a large amount of cash was taken; people are shot; or the robbers muffed their chance by making a quick stop in a men's room before the robbery. Banks categorically do not like publicity and they only divulge information about robberies — or, for that matter, any other problem — when the circumstances literally force them to.

It is virtually impossible to rob a bank and get a lot of money for your efforts: banks aren't dummies and they get especially nasty when someone tries to take their depositors' money. Robbers are especially dumb because they either don't know or don't care where most of the money is: it's sitting in the vault, not with the tellers.

The guard is the first person to show up for work at a bank. Generally, he gets to work at eight in the morning and then goes through a ritual which is right out of a grade B movie. Usually, the outside door of a bank has nothing but two simple locks, one at the top of the door and one at the bottom. There is nothing you can steal from a bank without getting into the vault, which is not opened until 8:45 A.M. Most banks today are designed in "bank moderne," which is a terrible school of architecture that is devoted to yards of plate glass windows so potential customers can look into the bank at night. (We once deviated from bank moderne by opening a marvelously designed bank that was on two levels connected by a sweeping staircase. At the cocktail party the night before the bank was to open, one of the senior officers, who has always been a bit of a lush, tried to negotiate the staircase, which unfortunately was so sweeping that it didn't have a banister to hang on to. He swayed momentarily, and then, to the dismay of everyone, plunged out of sight, like a fetid batch of pork bellies on the Commodities Exchange. The carpenters were in the bank the next day, putting in a banister, and that was the last time our design department tried anything but traditional, one-floor bank moderne.) Anyhow, our guard opens the branch, all by himself, at 8:00 sharp, and the first thing he does is to check that no one is in the bank. It is literally impossible to get into a bank without crashing through one of the glass windows, and those windows are so heavily wired to alarms that even the highest of junkie bank robbers knows enough not to try it. The guard walks through the entire bank, checking the vault area especially closely. If everything is satisfactory, he then sets up a signal to alert the rest of the employees that it's safe to enter the bank. The signal, which is made up by our signal committee (as differentiated from our vault committee and the thirty other committees we have humming away at First Mutual), can be a wastebasket overturned on a desk, or a cigarette burning in an ashtray, or a chair propped up against a desk — something simple, visual, prearranged, and, as I said, right off the old Warner Brothers' lot.

The rest of the staff of the branch, whom we hope have remembered what the week's signal is, see that everything is all clear around 8:30 A.M. and march on into work. I grant you, it's a bit like cops and robbers, but there it is, and who's to say that it doesn't serve a purpose?

If the employees start arriving, peer into the window, and don't see the sign or the guard, then there's trouble and they call the police who usually show up pronto. But to my knowledge this has never happened at our bank because no one in his right mind is going to get up at 8:00 A.M. and try to rob a bank — all he'll get is some cheap nylon carpeting and a few beat-up desks.

Opening the vault is a mystique all its own, a cross between *Doctor No* and the opening of "Get Smart," the television program that began with one set of doors opening to another set, and then still another set of doors.

Most banks today have a rather simple vault; practically all vaults have a locked gate outside, so the problem for the smart robber, the guy who knows he has to get into the vault to get money, is that he must open the locked gate first and then get into the vault. It's very difficult.

The entire setup is wired into the Holmes Protection Agency. The Holmes people are sitting in their office every day waiting for the all-clear signal. If, by chance, a bank robber has forced his way into the bank before 8:45 A.M., which is when the time lock on the vault opens, he has to force one of our guards to open the gate first. Naturally, the guard has a key; in fact, he has a key ring with dozens of keys which open doors to the teller area, to the bank itself, to men's rooms, and what have you. "Open the gate," says our robber. The guard can't wait to be of assistance. He takes out his key ring and selects a key for the gate. Unfortunately the robber has no way of knowing that there are indeed two keys to the gate: a normal gate key, and then a key we call a "spur key." The spur key opens the gate, but a tiny spur at the end of the key also activates a Holmes alarm. Presumably Holmes are wide awake, and when the alarm comes in they alert the police.

Beyond the gate is the vault. The vault has two combination locks on it, not unlike the locks used in gymnasiums. The two combination locks have, naturally, two separate combinations. These are changed weekly by the — right! — vault committee. The only person who has both sides of the combinations is the regional manager, who is the supervisor of the entire region that particular branch might be in. The two combinations are called the "official side" and the "clerical side," which is a very neat way banks have of letting their personnel know their status in the bank. Usually, the assistant manager has the combination to the clerical side and his superior, the branch manager, has the official side. The assistant manager goes into the vault in the morning, left —, right —, left —, right —; the manager does the same, and bingo, the vault opens. It is a very moving experience, but not nearly as emotional as the opening of the main vault in our downtown head-quarters. *That* takes approximately ten men.

After the vault is opened at 8:45 A.M., the *regular* Holmes alarm is set. (This Holmes alarm is not to be con-fused with the spur-key alarm built into the gate.) As you finish opening the vault and start walking toward the gate, you throw the Holmes switch on and then you buzz them. You are buzzing Holmes just to tell them everything is fine — and, need I say, there's a trick signal here, too. Each week, the Holmes okay signal is changed: i.e., it could be a buzz of two longs and a short, or any variation. If the per-son sending the okay signal to Holmes has a hangover and a shaky hand, the signal can be mistakenly sent and Holmes and the cops will be there in a jiffy.

Let us assume for a moment that one robber is brighter than most and he has forced his way into the bank and headed right for the vault. Let's also suppose that the gate is open and the vault is about to be closed at the end of the day when in pops a masked bandit. Since you don't have the opportunity to use the spur key and warn Holmes, what can you do?

One of the things you can do is to tell the robber politely — *very* politely — that you have to use the visible signal and let Holmes know that everything is going along swimmingly at the bank, that if you don't give the signal every cop within ten miles will be on the premises shortly. If the robber buys this piece of fiction, then you're sup-posed to send Holmes a false signal that there are robbers on the premises. Fat chance! You're standing at the wrong end of a shotgun frightened out of your skin, and it's probable that the robber is just as nervous as you are. (As for the robber with the bandana on his face whom I mentioned a bit earlier, the only thing to do would be to ask him if he needed to use a men's room.) The best bet is simply to invite the robber into the vault and let him wallow in money to his heart's content.

Another factor is that many people — and that includes bank employees — are terribly confused about the time lock on the vault. At 4:45 P.M., either the bank guard or the vault attendant goes into the vault to rewind the vault clock. As soon as the vault is shut, nothing in the world short of dynamite can open it until the clock goes off at the set time. Thus, at 4:45 P.M., the clock is wound and set sixteen hours ahead, so that it will open the vault at 8:45 the next morning. On Friday evening, before the weekend, the vault has to be wound for sixty-four hours, and where some of our people get confused is when they have to wind the clock with a holiday weekend coming up. Neither God nor any other force can budge that vault once it's set. We have had some embarrassing moments when the clock was wound erroneously, and the bank opened on time but the vault didn't. No vault, no bread, and we had to send out to another branch office for money to operate — a bit like "Give me $80,000 and hold the mayo."

Whenever you read about a bank robbery in the papers, be a little suspicious. Just the other day a West Side branch of a bank was hit for $35,000; one of the robbers was killed by the police, two others wounded, and twelve frightened customers who unfortunately happened to be in the bank at the time were briefly held as hostages. The papers expressed surprise that as soon as the firing between the police and the robbers began the customers hit the deck. If you live on the West Side and firing begins, falling to the ground is simply a natural reflex. The papers also said that "the tellers pressed the alarm," which summoned the police.

This is not quite accurate. Aside from the various alarms strewn about the vault and the vault gate, and the window and front door alarms, each teller's cash box is cunningly wired into either Holmes or the police. The decision to press the alarm is definitely not left up to the teller. If I were paid $115 a week and a bandito arrived seeking his fortune, I wouldn't press that alarm for all the money in the world. Banks understand this desire for self-preservation in all of us. What they've devised is a simple clip device at the bottom of each teller's cash box. When the teller goes to the vault each morning to get her day's supply of money, the bills are placed in a metal drawer. The clip goes over the last bill in the stack; when the entire stack of money is removed, the clip is activated, setting off a silent alarm which rings at Holmes and also triggering the cameras that are placed throughout the bank. When the robber says, "This is a stickup and give me your money," all the teller need do is comply. Give him all the money, and as the last bill leaves the cash drawer the alarm and cameras begin.

You would think that with all this protection people would wise up and get out of the bank robbery business. The statistics, however, don't show it. In 1969, there were 139 robberies in the metropolitan New York area, but in 1970 the figure increased to 469. Roughly a fifth of the nation's bank robberies occur in New York; the nationwide figure for 1970 approached 2,300. When you look at the money that the robbers took, it seems like a futile business to be in.

As far as the amount of money stolen, it is very little indeed. For example, in the first three months of 1971 there were 36 attempts at bank robbery, and of the 36 only 17 were successful. The total loss in the 17 holdups which succeeded was $191,000, or about $11,250 per robbery. The courts are now handing out terms ranging from ten years in prison on up, and no matter how you look at the mathematics, the money just isn't enough to make it worthwhile.

The banks install new security measures, and sure enough, the robbers come up with a countermeasure. Not only do we have cameras triggered when a robbery is in progress, but some banks have installed elaborate videotape-camera equipment, which takes a photograph of the entire banking floor every thirty seconds; no matter what occurs, the bank has a complete visual record of whoever attempts a robbery. The robbers, fully aware of the camera equipment, have resorted to spraying the camera lenses with paint from aerosol paint sprays during a robbery.

Most authorities agree that it is much safer, if there is such a word, to deal with a professional rather than an amateur robber. The most dangerous of all amateurs are the drug addicts, whose behavior is absolutely unpredictable. Some amateur bank robbers walk into a bank and ask for a specific amount: perhaps it's their rent, or the amount of money they owe to a finance company. One day last spring a robber walked into one of our uptown branches and demanded that the manager hand over $5,000. Our manager replied, with what I consider staggering sangfroid, "Will you take $2,000?" The robber said, "Yes," and took the money and ran. To my knowledge it was the first negotiated bank robbery on record, and it may well bring a host of innovations in the bank robbery field.

Needless to say, bank robbery per se is an art form that the Federal Bureau of Investigation has spent a considerable amount of time and energy studying. Since the days of Dillinger, one of the favorite pursuits of the FBI (aside from Communists) has been the bank robber and, by and large, in this area they have shown a great amount of expertise. The FBI studied several hundred bank robberies over a two-year period and determined that the most popular day for bank robberies is Friday (payday), and the most frequent time span on Friday is between 12 noon and 2 P.M.

The study says that there is no such thing as a typical robber or robbery, which I think is probably true. The survey also showed that half of the robberies studied occurred in branch offices situated in downtown fringe areas or in the suburbs. Logically, this makes sense, because with traffic jams being what they are, it would be madness to try and rob a bank on Wall Street or Fifth Avenue — you just couldn't get away.

Our branch location department once put up a lovely bank out on Long Island, all shiny glass and sparkling, away from the soot and filth of New York City. Unfortunately, they built the damned bank about sixty yards from an entrance to the Long Island Expressway. This branch has been open for two years, and it has been robbed five times already. Robbers are quite perceptive in the access road sector, and when they see our branch sitting in the middle of nowhere, just a stone's throw from an expressway where they can get away at seventy-five miles an hour, they take advantage of you.

I've talked to some of the personnel in that branch, and by now they're inured to robberies: "Well, just another robbery." During the most recent robbery, the robbers came in and asked, "Is the vault open?" The manager of the branch unfortunately happened to be chatting with his area supervisor. I've no doubt that if he had been by himself he would have said that indeed the vault was wide open, be our guest. However, with the boss peering over your shoulder, you tend to play the corporate game. The manager said, "Oh, no, the vault is locked," and fortunately for everyone the robbers took his word. The vault was wide open, but because so many of us are not particularly familiar with what an open vault even looks like, the robbers failed to recognize that they were passing up $100,000 in cash. They were satisfied with what they got from the tellers and then off they zoomed on the expressway. (For those of you who have spent hours in traffic jams on the Long Island Expressway, let me point out that the branch is very far out on Long Island, thus the relative ease that robbers have in traveling on it.)

In the FBI study they found that 1,400 of the offenders entered the bank through the front door, which sounds logical enough. On the other hand, 178 came through the rear door, 91 through a side door, and 4 came through the roof. Why a bank robber would take the trouble to come through the roof is beyond me.

The problem of disguises is a difficult one for bankers to sort out; all you have to do is walk down the main street of any city in the world to see how people are dressing to grasp the problem. Stand in a bank for fifteen minutes or so and you'll see people in business suits, freaks in long hair, transvestites, rock stars dragging their guitars behind them. If a hippie, hung with beads and swirling in incense, walks up to a teller's window in bare feet, for all we know he's about to rob us or deposit $10,000 — the proceeds of a hashish run to Morocco. Today there is no such thing as being dressed out of the ordinary, and those wonderful days of yesteryear when robbers wore something as simple as a stocking over the head or a Halloween mask are gone forever. In New York and London, the capitals of sartorial nonconformity, there are fairly rational people walking the streets with involved air filter masks on their faces — the masks supposedly eliminate the toxic parts of the air we breathe. Up on Madison Avenue there is a famous Japanese lady who has been wearing a white gauze mask for years. Her specialty is getting on the Madison Avenue bus and then emptying it because she's always muttering Asiatic imprecations to herself.

The FBI acknowledges this problem: in their survey they found that in practically all robberies disguises were used, including sunglasses, false beards, ski masks, Halloween masks, tape or gauze on their faces, falls (as in a woman's hair fall), hoods, shawls, capes, wigs, and last, but certainly not least, full-scale out-and-out drag.

In one drag case, the gunman was tastefully attired in a blond wig, red skirt, black hose, woman's coat, stylish purse, and a Smith & Wesson — the 38-caliber model. He walked into a savings and loan association (and their money is as good as ours), stepped up to the teller, put his purse on the counter, opened it, and brought out a note demanding $1,000. The teller gave him the money and he fled. When the police arrived they flooded the area and soon learned that a woman had just dashed into an all-male boarding house. In the robber's room they caught him with his skirt down, as it were, and in fact he still was wearing his black stockings under his trousers. The money and the gun were under his pillow.

Most of the bank robbers covered in the FBI survey were between the ages of twenty-six and thirty-six and of either medium or slender build. Four of the robbers had leg amputations, eleven had missing fingers, nine were toothless (which must have made the archetypal "Hand over the money" next to impossible), two had snow white hair, nine had crippled limbs, the oldest was a veteran of sixty-eight, the youngest was a high-school senior proving to his buddies that he wasn't afraid to rob a bank, and two of the robbers were blind. Not partially blind, not impaired vision, not failing vision — but blind. The mind boggles at the logistics those two had to go through to rob their banks.

The most difficult robberies to prevent are those in which the robbery is compounded with a kidnapping; i.e., the robber takes a hostage or hostages. Although these robberies have a slightly better chance of succeeding, the robber is really running a greater risk because the penalty for kidnapping in many states is either life imprisonment or death. A year ago in New York three masked robbers kidnapped a bank executive and held him overnight on Staten Island along with thirteen of his friends and relatives. The next day, they forced him at gunpoint to hand over $250,-000 from his bank, Community National of Brooklyn. Two of the three were subsequently caught.

The FBI survey details one robber who made a specialty of kidnapping bank officials. His method of operation was to walk into a bank and ask to see the manager, saying that his business was confidential. Usually he was taken to a conference room and that's when he'd pull out his gun. He'd tell the manager to prepare a cashier's check for $10,000 and have it cashed, and then, on the pretext of taking the manager out for coffee, he'd drive away in the manager's car. With the manager. Someplace along the line he'd drop off the bank official, and then he'd abandon the official's car to pick his own car up.

This robber managed to pull off four such robberies before he got caught. All four robberies took place in a small town; they are geared to a small-town bank. In New York or Chicago there's little if any confidential business conducted away from an officer's desk. You wouldn't stand a chance of pulling such a stunt off in one of our banks; our managers are usually away trying to drum up customers, telling people how safe it is for them to have their money in our bank.

Fortunately, we've never had a kidnapping at any of our banks. The closest we've come was a job that took place out in Brooklyn, where the robber called the bank and demanded to speak to the manager. When he got him on the phone, the robber said that he was holding the man's wife as a hostage and he wanted the manager to show up at a certain street corner with a specified amount of money. The manager called his home and his wife answered the telephone. Then the manager called the police and the robber was grabbed. But what if his wife had been out shopping or away for the day? Undoubtedly the manager would have had to turn over the money.

By and large, most bank robbers use guns or toy guns, and most of them use handwritten notes saying simply

"Give me $———." The FBI did uncover one shrewd robber who went to various skid rows and would talk someone down on his luck into performing the actual robbery while he waited outside in the getaway car. He got away with this technique for at least twenty robberies.

But here again I'm afraid the FBI is talking about a type of robbery that might work in, say, Des Moines, but certainly not in New York City. First, your average man off the Bowery in New York is so marinated in muscatel that the odds are he couldn't walk steadily into any bank, much less turn over a note and negotiate his way out of the bank. Even if the man you got off the Bowery were sober enough to talk to, knowing the New York *panache,* the odds are that the Boweryite would try to chisel the instigator, or at least try to figure out a hustler's angle.

The New York Clearing House Association, which is made up of eleven major banks and their branches in the Greater New York area, started a policy of offering a $10,000 reward for the apprehension and conviction of bank robbers. The association has put up posters in all of the major banks, depicting a bundle of bank robbers. Those who have been caught are very dramatically x-ed out on the poster. One of the robbers, a man named Raymond Hendrickson, had been wanted for robbing a Queens bank. When he saw his name on the posters, he called the FBI. "Come and get me," he is reported to have said. "I'm not going to let any of my friends make $10,000 on me."

Although the FBI doesn't say so, I can say with some certainty that most bank robbers most of the time are poor people in desperate circumstances. Not only is this ascertainable by their demands — $582, $1,092, etc. — but because only a desperate man would try to rob a bank.

The most spectacular scores are really not pulled off in bank robberies. In this country and abroad, the gigantic robberies are made when large amounts of money are moved to and from a bank. Thus, the Brinks armored car company has provided robbers with amounts ranging above $1,000,000, and of course the Great Train Robbery in Great Britain also involved huge amounts of money.

As for banks per se, the odds are way against the robber. The security systems are too good; the alarm systems are constantly being improved until they've reached the point where they're almost foolproof. The only time I've ever heard of one of the alarms not being foolproof was during an incident at the Chase Manhattan Bank. Chase, like other major New York banks, handles the distribution of food stamps to people on welfare. At one of the Chase branches, the line was long, the day was hot, and the people in line began to get restive. Sure enough, two of the women in line began fighting with each other and one woman completely ripped the blouse off the other. One of the tellers became so agitated that she somehow tripped the silent alarm, and not only did the police arrive, but the cameras began recording the entire scene for posterity. The film of the riot is reportedly available for viewing at Chase.

# CHAPTER II

ONE day at one of our Manhattan branches, a well-dressed, affable, pleasant, well-spoken man walked up to a teller's window with a $1,000 check to cash. The check had been drawn a few days before, on the Trust Company of New Jersey — the Hoboken branch — and it was made out to the fellow who was trying to cash it. His name — at least on the check — was George Gershwin. The teller, a pimply, gum-chewing, $95-a-week girl, who might have been all of twenty-one, did not have the slightest idea that George Gershwin was a Golden Oldie. Her ventures into musicology extended to Mick Jagger and no further.

Before the teller could say a word, George Gershwin quickly pointed out that he had an account at First Mutual Trust Company, not at this particular branch but rather at a Brooklyn branch. He had thoughtfully put his account number on the back of the check. He also pointed out to the teller that the check already had been given an "okay to cash" by a platform officer, and lo and behold, there was the signature of an officer. The teller asked George who had okayed the check and George said "Mr. Jones, he's sitting right over there." The teller looked over to the platform and saw Mr. Jones, took a hasty look again at the "okay to cash" and saw that it, too, was Mr. Jones's. Then George interjected a little patter into his act and said, "You're new here, aren't you?" And before the teller could answer him George continued, "Miss Baker [another teller] also knows me." The teller looked down toward Miss Baker's cage and saw that she was not there; then the teller cashed the check. Rhapsody in Green!

Jersey George Gershwin was a swindler, and into the general category of swindles fall all manner of check forgeries, check kiting, and phony schemes of one sort or another. As differentiated from out-and-out bank robberies, swindles require a bit more than muscle: nerve, intelligence, adaptability. Your average swindler is a cut above the average bank robber: your sister might end up marrying a swindler without your knowing it.

It's not hard to predict what happened to George Gershwin's check. It went through the New York Clearing House and was sent to Hoboken for collection, whereupon it bounced rapidly back to us. At this point someone higher up than the teller took a look at the check and then held his head in despair. When the security and auditing people got around to questioning the teller, she asked how she was supposed to know that George Gershwin was not around, all she knew was that George Gershwin was well dressed, pleasant, and he "talked nice."

I'd be pleasant and talk nice, too, if I had as many ASCAP songs going for me as George Gershwin does. The current George Gershwin obviously was a pretty smart fellow. He had cased the bank on previous occasions and had probably gone to one of the platform officers to have a legitimate check approved. He also knew enough to realize that tellers go on and off duty fairly frequently. And he probably had practiced forging the "okay to cash" of Mr. Jones enough times to risk cashing the check.

The girl who cashed the check was named Miss Rodriguez and her basic problem was stupidity. If a man walked up to a teller's window with a $1,000 check to cash he normally wouldn't have had the "okay to cash" on the check. The teller would have taken a look at the size of the check and then referred the man to an officer for the approval. So the teller should have been wary of the "okay to cash" already on the check. Second, the customer started a conversation while the teller was counting out the $1,000. Every legitimate customer of every bank in the world knows not to start a distracting conversation while someone is counting out *your* money. Such a conversation is always the sign that something is wrong.

And, of course, the alias. Why the man risked using George Gershwin is beyond me; he might have been safer with Irving Berlin, or perhaps Cole Porter. Gershwin was taking a chance that the teller, no matter how young she might have appeared, could have recognized the name George Gershwin and blown the whistle. Also, the teller was lazy. Miss Rodriguez, having been told by Gershwin that he had an account at a branch in Brooklyn, simply could have verified it by looking at the account listings or by making a phone call.

If she had been brighter and less lazy, she could have asked him one pertinent question and he would have walked away. Because he was a professional, he probably would have said, "Oh, never mind, I've decided not to cash my check. Just give it back to me." Out he would have gone. I should point out that a risky transaction is no less risky if the person attempting it is charming and well dressed. Most of the tellers who commit a blunder such as this tell the security people, "But he was so very nice and well dressed." Our best crooks are charming and well dressed.

In the Gershwin case, the auditors came in and talked to Miss Rodriguez, and if they didn't scare the wits out of her the FBI will someday do the job. In the discussions with Miss Rodriguez the bank decided to keep her on as a teller because she was a trainee.

Why do we have trainees in situations like this? Because we don't pay our tellers enough and our turnover in non-management personnel is over 50 percent a year. We're practically sweeping the streets to fill these $95-a-week (less federal, state, and city withholding taxes) positions, and when a Miss Rodriguez lands on our beach she simply is too unsophisticated and too inexperienced to handle her job. More to the point, she probably doesn't give a damn.

We kept Miss Rodriguez on, figuring that she would learn a lesson from the experience — and that the other tellers would, too. Naturally, we were wrong. One month later Miss Rodriguez failed to prove out (the amount of cash that went out of her window in one day was $125 more than she took in). In bank terminology, an amount of $125 is called a "nonsatisfactory difference," meaning that it is not particularly above suspicion.

Despite the $1,000 to George Gershwin and the short of $125, the personnel department and the manager of her branch decided to give her one more chance and she was kept on as a teller.

Consider, if you will, a swindler who called himself "Schroeder" and was described in the bulletins subsequently put out on him as "male, white, about twenty-five years of age, with a bushy haircut and a large amount of hair on the front of his head, and wearing a goatee." On any given day you can walk down Fifth Avenue in New York and see a dozen "Schroeders." This particular Schroeder was a coin swindler. He walked into one of the branches of our bank with twenty-two rolls of dimes all neatly wrapped up and Scotch-taped, with a savings account number printed on the wrapper. He told the teller that he had a savings account at the branch and wanted to exchange his twenty-two rolls of dimes for $110 in cash. The teller didn't bother to see if Schroeder had an account at the bank, much less open up even one of the rolls to see if there were dimes there. Needless to say, the rolls didn't contain fifty dimes to a roll, but rather forty-one pennies a roll. Schroeder had a consummate amount of gall in that he didn't even waste one dime at the end of the roll in case the teller might have checked just one of the twenty-two rolls. We weren't the only ones who got clipped by Schroeder; he managed to unload eighty-eight rolls on various branches of Chase Manhattan.

There is no explanation for the case. Later, when questioned about the transaction, the teller said that he was suspicious about Schroeder's appearance but did nothing about it. I don't really know what is going on in tellers' minds when something like this happens. Maybe they're thinking about lunch, or maybe they've just finished lunch and they are logy, or perhaps they're stir crazy. Plus, it's not their money so they don't care. The result: we lost $100.98. (We did salvage the pennies that Schroeder left with us.)

Strange things sometimes happen to coins. Here's a charming memorandum from our files:

"Dry Dock Savings Bank made a cash deposit of $999.77. This deposit consisted of several bags of loose coin. This money was delivered from Dry Dock Savings Bank in their own station wagon driven by their armed guard 'and brought into the bank by a clerk who accompanies the guard. The money was taken from the station wagon to our vault to be rolled and the clerk brought the deposit ticket up to teller Alan Williams to be receipted. This was done without the teller checking the deposit. . . ."

Anger in Dry Dock Country. After the money was rolled, the vault custodian, who had originally accepted the money, brought the rolled coins upstairs to the teller; a bag of dimes worth $200.20 was missing. We never did find the missing bag of dimes — it always seems to be dimes — but it obviously disappeared on our premises and the folks over at friendly Dry Dock were a little put out. Thereafter, whenever Dry Dock arrived with a deposit of coins, they were brought directly to the teller area and counted.

We get taken for large amounts and small in every imaginable way. One April, a teller of ours blithely cashed a check drawn on another bank for a woman who said she was an employee of the bank — First Mutual Trust employee chatting casually with First Mutual Trust teller. Only $40. It took two days for the check to bounce. When we talked to the teller, she said the person posing as our employee had even gone so far as to put her employee number on the back of the bad check. The teller also said she could not recall if the woman had shown her official identification or not, or even if she had seen her in the bank before. Ah well, charge another $40 to "accounts receivable," except that we will never receive that $40. Three months later, in July, the same teller cashed a $110.50 check drawn by an imaginary corporation and endorsed by an equally imaginary man named Gordon. In her words, the man who cashed the check was someone who was known to her as a signer on an account or a person who regularly made deposits for "someone." According to the memo put out on this check, the teller "will continue to try to identify the individual." How? By walking the streets looking for someone named Gordon? Meanwhile, let's charge it up to good old "accounts receivable." What knocks me out is the fifty cents on the check. As for the teller, who knows where she is today? The odds are that she's been promoted to the platform as an officer.

Sometimes swindles are deceptively simple. A young man once walked into one of our branches, strode right over to the platform and talked to one of the officers. He identified himself as the grandson of Mrs. X. Mrs. X has a Custodian Account with us and Mrs. X's money is significant money — meaning that any grandson of Mrs. X is someone we treat politely. The young man's name was Herman and his story was that he attended college in Germany, that he was on his way home for a visit but that he needed $75, and could we cash his check drawn on his German bank. Unfortunately, he didn't happen to have any checks from his German bank so he would have to use one of our blank checks. His parents, by the way, lived in Atlanta, but don't try to contact them, he said, because they're on a cruise. This was in mid-October and, needless to say, it took a little time, but by November the check went to Germany for collection and it took a cruise of its own, returning to us with the notation "unable to locate drawee bank." The officer finally located the parents the day the check bounced, and they informed him that Herman indeed was their son and indeed was Mrs. X's grandson, but Herman was a black sheep and the parents, frankly, were fed up with him. They said that Herman wasn't attending college in Germany; instead, he was AWOL from the army in Germany, which, according to Mom, had caused the Armed Forces Police and the FBI to be interested in Herman's whereabouts. Mom also said, politely but firmly, that Herman had hung some $2,000 in bad paper hither and yon and she wasn't about to make good any of the checks. As for Grandma, the less said the better.

If our bank seems to be overloaded with tellers who are continually out for a beer, our officers don't set much of an example either. The officer in this case should be stuffed and sold as day-old wurst. There were a number of things he could have done. First, despite the story, he could have called Herman's home in Atlanta simply to verify that Herman was the son. Second, he should have called Grandmother X to confirm that Herman was her grandson. Third, he should have looked at Polk's *World Bank Directory;* at least *some* attempt to verify the bank could have been made. But officers of our bank are inflicted with the same glorious descriptive powers that our hapless tellers have. The officer who approved Herman's check said that he "was well dressed and well spoken." There is a slight difference and one which neatly stratifies and codifies the officer. Officers would say "well spoken"; a teller would say "he spoke well." It doesn't matter, naturally, since well-spoken Herman got away.

Herman hopped right over to the platform and sought out an officer. But in most forgery-cum-fraud-cum-swindles the swindler never makes it to the platform: he does his job on the luckless teller and runs. For example, this typical split deposit.

(A word about split deposits, which take place when you cash part of a check drawn to you and then deposit the rest of the check to your account. All of us have made split deposits at one time or another, especially with paychecks, where you might deposit $350 to your checking account and keep $50 cash. Split deposits are fertile territory for the swindler; the busy and deficient teller makes an a priori assumption that since the person is depositing some money in an account, it is a better risk to give him cash in return than to take a chance and cash the entire check and turn over all the money. Tellers may be stupid, but swindlers aren't, and they know the psychological advantage of presenting a check to a teller with a deposit slip made out partly for deposit and the remainder for cash. The best of the swindlers aren't greedy; they keep the proportion between deposit and cash sensible, so you rarely see a case of a split deposit fraud where 95 percent of the check was for cash and only 5 percent was for deposit.)

Anyhow, a customer came into our main office with a $469 check, of which he deposited $150 and planned to keep $319 in cash. The check was drawn by three men whose first names were Herbert, Frank, and Irving (an unlikely trio) on the Royal State Bank of New York. The teller evidently was impressed by Herbert, Frank, and Irving, because she automatically cashed the check without referring it to the platform; seven days later it automatically bounced from Royal State with the notation that Herbert,

Frank, and Irving at one time did have an account with Royal State but no more. And Royal State did not have any further information about where Herbert, Frank, or Irving could be found.

Because this particular bad check bounced at the headquarters of our bank there was more than the usual consternation. After all, one assumes that only the crème de la crème are working at headquarters: out in the boondocks of Brooklyn the crude natives might make such a gaffe, but at headquarters, never. Immediately, a cloud of officers descended on the teller. She simply shrugged and said she cashed the check because it looked like a payroll check. The officer writing the report then continued in rather broken English to say: "and being the customer endorsed it with his name and account number she thought it was in order, never bothering to refer it to the platform." The officer then added a handwritten footnote to his little epistle in which he said, "Even though she is aware that such a transaction should be referred to the platform, she thought this particular transaction was all right for her to handle on her own. That is the only explanation she could give. Howard Ewald assured me Miss Kaminsky will not make such a mistake in the future. (I hope not!)" Don't you love that "I hope not!"? An officer of one of the largest banks in the world is keeping his fingers crossed.

In fairness to officers on the platform who have to okay checks under pressure (here again the swindler is well aware of the familiar image of the disgruntled, time-pressed customer waiting approval of his check), the bank doesn't make life any easier for them.

Not long ago a memo was circulated throughout the bank — and I assume to all banks in the metropolitan area

— which was a "guide" to spotting counterfeit New York drivers' licenses. Here is the example used; the memo adds that if any of the tests fail, the license is counterfeit.

*Example:* The individual's name is Sopkin and his date of birth is 8/17/32. License #S15538 13942 395384-32.
1. The letter preceding the number is the first letter of the individual's last name, i.e., *S*.
2. The second two numbers (circled) are the number of the second letter of the last name, i.e. *O*, 15th letter of the alphabet. (If second letter was *E*, the number would be 05.)
3. The second set of circled numbers is arrived at as follows:

   63 × month of birth, i.e., 63 × 8 = 504
   plus
   2 × date of birth    2 × 17 = $\frac{34}{538}$

   If the license holder is a woman, you add one to the above number.
4. The last two numbers are the year of birth of the license holder.

If you're a resident of New York State and have a driver's license, try working out this nifty exercise in less than five minutes. And while you're doing it, picture fifteen people clamoring for attention at the platform. After you've solved the problem and your license conforms, ponder the final sentence of the memorandum: "It does not mean it could not be a counterfeit, and all other usual cautions should be exercised." In other words, make sure the customer is well dressed and well spoken.

By their very nature, check swindles are usually for relatively small amounts of money — a $150 check here, $630 there. Not to say that it doesn't add up. Last year we had over $600,000 charged off to bad debt, thousands of small larcenies which add up to a large headache. When a swindler tries to sneak a $2,000 check by us he usually will be caught. Tellers don't casually cash checks for that amount. Under normal circumstances those checks automatically go to the platform for approval.

Fortunately, we've never been hit with an enormous swindle, though I don't know which is worse: thousands of small swindles yearly or one gigantic swindle which can wipe you out in an instant. Banks are not proud of swindles, and you rarely hear about them from either your colleagues in banking or from reading the papers. In the last two years the only major swindle that has crept into the papers (albeit the *New York Daily News*) was a gorgeous flim-flam pulled on Bankers Trust Company and the National Bank of North America. A man named Salvatore Giordano and his two brothers, Anthony and John, evidently working in cahoots with two bank officers, one from each of the banks, were able to get away with almost $900,000 in just over a two-year period. They managed it through what is called check kiting.

What they did was to work out a system whereby deposits made by the Giordano boys (one of whom, by the way, ran a harness-racing stable) were immediately treated as cash. Let me explain, if I can. When you walk into your bank with a personal check from a friend, you can't safely draw against that check until it has cleared your friend's bank. Depending on where his bank is, this might well take from four to ten days. If you've no other funds in the bank, you cannot draw on your friend's check, for fear your own check will bounce for insufficient funds. *However,* if your check is approved as a cash deposit by an officer this is a different story, *mia cara.*

To further elucidate: If you walk into a bank with a $25,000 check, it can be deposited to your account, but the bookkeeping department will have that check flagged, allowing no other checks to be drawn against it. But if that check of yours is okayed by the assistant manager of a bank as a cash deposit, when it is deposited it is immediately posted to your balance as cash; you can start cashing other checks against it immediately. The Giordano boys were very clever, in that they had two bank officers working with them, according to the indictment.

Let us assume that the original $25,000 check was a bummer, not worth the paper it was written on. To start the check-kiting cycle rolling, one of the bank officers okayed it as cash. Although that check was okayed, it eventually is going to bounce unless it is somehow covered. That is, even though two officers from two banks are working in the scheme, that $25,000 check will inevitably show up as bad. For the sake of argument, let's say that you cash a $5,000 check against the $25,000 deposit, which you can do because that original check is still okay. However, you've got to deposit another $25,000 check to cover the initial deposit. It, too, is a phony, but it, too, is treated as a cash deposit, and so when the first bad check comes home sure enough there is cash, which presumably was used by the Giordano *fratelli* to pay the feed bills for their horsies.

All of these checks were drawn on either Bankers Trust or National Bank, and each time they bounced back and forth between the two banks the perpetrators raised the amounts. According to the papers, checks totaling over $50 million were written and all hands managed to siphon off $887,000. The paperwork involved in this swindle is hard to contemplate: after all, it went on for over two years and the transactions were limited to just the two participating banks. Notice that even though $50 million in checks was written, the total boodle from the operation amounted to only a bit less than $900,000. Put another way, less than 2 percent of the face value of the checks written ended up as loot. Therefore, the gang only raised the checks about 2 percent each time, which is the way a first class check-kiting operation should work.

This swindle all fell apart because of one dumb bank messenger, who neglected to take a bundle of checks from the Bankers Trust branch where the swindle was going merrily along to the main branch. Those checks must have been crucial to the operation, because when they did not arrive the Giordano accounts showed up $440,000 short on Monday morning. No bank lets any account casually run a half million dollars short. An investigation was started immediately and everyone was caught.

The smart part of the operation was that the Giordanos managed to get two bank officers working with them. Where they could have improved upon their scheme was to get a third bank into the act, and along with the third bank, a third officer. Because when you're kiting checks between Banks A, B, and C, the additional bank gives you an additional three days or so for a margin of safety. Their big failure was to think that the operation could go on forever. Nothing goes on forever, not even a scheme as well planned as this one. That the entire thing blew sky high because of one messenger who forgot to pick up a bundle of checks is a good example of the many things which can and will go wrong.

I don't know what the individual banks did after the scheme was uncovered, but my assumption is that each bank transferred every person in the branch involved. When an operation of this size and magnitude is busted, the theory is, clean house and start with brand new personnel. I'm also curious about how National Bank and Bankers Trust managed to bury the loss. Banks have to work very hard to make a profit of $887,000, and when that kind of money floats out the window the auditors must be very creative. At First Mutual Trust Company we would have called the loss "unresolved differences" and held our breath.

My guess is that if the indictments were handed down on a Thursday, then on the following morning the headquarters of each of the banks involved was humming. What we would have done would have been to replace everybody and everything — new people from top to bottom (and that includes secretaries), new combinations on every lock in the place, new sets of credentials — and an entire new look.

The rationale for all this is guilt by association. For example, one of the bank officers caught was an assistant manager of a branch — and yet I'll bet that the manager of the branch was removed from his job not because he was implicated in the swindle, but because he was neglectful or unlucky enough to have it happen under his jurisdiction. And when they fire the manager the bank quietly lets other banks know that although this fellow didn't get indicted by a grand jury, he was responsible, so to speak, and he probably will have to find another job in another profession. As for the messenger who unwittingly caused the discovery of the entire mess, he undoubtedly got yelled at for forgetting to deliver the bag of checks.

Check kiting is complicated; check forgery in all of its infinite variations is much simpler. Here's a gentleman who hit several New York, Long Island, and Wisconsin banks with a certified-check forgery technique which isn't startlingly new, but it sure is effective. Incidentally, he called himself Thomas Watson, and although he hasn't done as well as his namesake at IBM, he's managed to do pretty well. The bulletin put out to all New York banks on Watson said,

Individual who is described as male, black, height 5'9", age 28 or 29 years. Clean-shaven face, medium-brown skin, well dressed, wearing black frame glasses, well spoken, well mannered; who opens a special checking account with a small amount of cash and then certifies checks in the amount of $21, $22, $23, and $24. The checks are so prepared that, after the figure is written, the word "and" is changed to "hundred" and the certified check is raised to $2,000-odd. The raised certified check is then presented, usually at a branch of the same bank, for encashment.

When you walk into your bank and have a check certified, the teller calls down to operations and immediately has the amount of the certified check transferred out of your checking account into the certification account, where it is held in abeyance until the certified check comes through for collection. So when Thomas Watson certified a check for $21 the teller would check the balance in his account (his balance very shrewdly always held at least $21). This amount was transferred into the certification account, and the check for $21 was certified by the bank. (A certified check is the next best thing to cash. It is negotiable, treated as cash, and not scrutinized as carefully as it should be.) What Watson then did was to raise the certified check, in just the same well-spoken way described in the interbank memo. He was then the proud possessor of a $2,100 certified check, and because he was very professional, he never attempted to cash it for its entire face value. He usually went to a branch of the same bank and made a split deposit, putting $1,400 into his special checking account and keeping $700 in cash. Since the money is safely put away when the check is certified, Watson had this going for him when passing his forged certified checks. Ninety-nine out of a hundred tellers would treat just like cash a deposit made with a certified check.

Assuming that Mr. Watson was successful enough to own a car and smart enough to know the location of branches of banks in the metropolitan New York area, he could, if he didn't hit too much traffic, get his hands on about $10,000 in a given day. (I am figuring that he got $700 per forged check and passed roughly fifteen of these on fifteen different branches.) One would also assume that since Mr. Watson originally opened his own special checking account, he's got some sort of false identification, enough identification to deposit these checks without raising too many questions. Here again, tellers have encashment limits — usually $500 — and even though Watson has an account at a different branch of the bank and even though he's got a certified check, the split deposit of $2,100 should be referred to an officer. One telephone call and you would discover in a minute that certification is holding $21, not $2,100.

But the tellers are busy, the lines are long, the check *is* certified, it *is* a split deposit, there *is* an account, so why not? When a certified check is cashed, it doesn't follow the usual path of a check being cashed. Normally, a check goes through the bookkeeping department, where it is posted to the account. But a certified check, coming from a branch, bypasses the bookkeepers and goes straight to the certification account where the check number and the amount are immediately compared with the money being held against the certified check. The certification account is holding a fast $21 and here comes a certified check for $2,100 — and it doesn't take a computer programmer to figure out that something is amiss. By the time the certification department starts to scream, Thomas Watson is on his merry — and well-spoken — way.

It usually takes a day and a half for a certified check to work its way back through a branch to the certified accounts. Although this is at least a day quicker than a normal check, it does give Watson time to hit and run.

In my opinion, Watson, who must have worked at a bank at some point in his career, has devised himself a pretty good scheme. He is dealing with the certified check, which, while it isn't sacrosanct, is one step up from the normal check. Most tellers are wary enough to raise a flag of warning when they're presented with a forged check, but a certified check has an aura of respectability about it. It has the imprimatur of the bank upon it; it stands for a document that the bank has scrutinized to a certain degree. Of course when a Thomas Watson hits a city and the bad certified checks start falling like leaves, the banks start issuing interbank memoranda and sooner or later they'll catch Watson if he doesn't leave town. But the truly bright swindler knows enough to leave in a few days. When we got the bulletin on Thomas Watson he had already zipped through Milwaukee, Long Island, and Manhattan, and I'm positive he left town after picking up his $10,000 or so.

Do we ever run to ground the Thomas Watsons of the world? Of course we do, but there are no statistics to show how effective or ineffective we are. Certainly we could institute a policy whereby every certified check presented for encashment must be cleared either with the platform or by telephone with the certification department, but that defeats the purpose of a certified check, which is supposed to be regarded as cash. Naturally we'll keep our eyes out for Watson, but I think that's a hopeless task.

Fortunately for us, the Thomas Watsons of this world are in a minority. On the other hand, there are literally dozens of Variations on a Theme by Thomas Watson, and one of the most frequent is the New York–California–New York Movement. Essentially, the swindler walks into a bank and says that he's just moved to horrible, crime-ridden New York and he wants to open an account. (California officials play this back when the potential customer strolls in to Wells Fargo or Bank of America, removes his new sunglasses and says he's just left crime-ridden New York and wants to establish an account and credit in sunny, funny California.)

A gentleman bounced into one of our branches, announced that he was from Pomona, and opened a savings account with a cash deposit of $25. Because, like all banks, we want to get our hands on every bit of loose, floating cash, we quickly went through all the forms and opened an account for Mr. Able. What the platform officer didn't do, though, was to run a check on Mr. Able as soon as he opened the account. Mr. Able is a transient (he turned out to be one hell of a transient), and accounts opened by transients should be given special handling. Someone should have checked his address, his new job in terrible New York, and made sure that his California driver's license hadn't been purchased from an aging beach boy in Santa Monica. The point is that initial reference and document checking often prevents cash loss later on. Mr. Able, according to the description fuzzily recalled by everyone months later, was neat, well dressed, and well spoken — the holy trio. There are very few legitimate citizens from California who, on moving to New York, start a relationship with a bank by an initial deposit of *only* $25 and a savings account at that; they would have more need for a checking account. The amount in itself is a warning sign and it should have been flagged by either the officer handling the new account or the teller.

Mr. Able opened his savings account on May 2 and two days later made a withdrawal of $20, leaving a balance of $5. Another warning flag ignored by all and sundry. Not only did the well-dressed new arrival to our shores start his account with a suspiciously small amount of cash, just two days later, on May 4, he withdrew four-fifths of it. Someone should have noticed that on the monthly account printouts, which give account activity on every account in the branch. From May 4 until July 13, two and a half months after his first withdrawal, the account remained dormant. No deposits or withdrawals. But on July 13, things began to happen.

Into another branch walked Mr. Able and made an interoffice deposit to his savings account for $1,100, which is considerably more than $25, and, what's more, in the form of a check drawn on a California bank. The credit slip, indicating a check deposit to the savings account, was received the following day by the original branch where Mr. Able had been doing business. So far, Mr. Able had a savings account balance of $1,105. On July 20, seven days after the deposit of $1,100 (there's usually a ten-day waiting period for California checks to clear), Mr. Able walked into the branch where he had his savings account and cashed a personal check made out to him for $600. Although he didn't have a checking account with us, he forthrightly presented his savings passbook with its $1,105 balance. While he was cashing the $600 check, he also was busily depositing a $475 check to the savings account, which brought his savings account balance up to $1,580. The teller, ignoring her encashment limit of $500, went cheerfully ahead and cashed the $600 check. She did remember to call the operations people and put a hold on the account for $600, meaning that $600 was immediately pulled out of the savings account to be held in case the $600 check proved to be rubbery. The fallacy, naturally, was that the original $1,100 check still hadn't cleared through the California bank; thus, the savings account balance of $1,580 was so much smog.

On July 25, all of the bad checks began coming home to roost. The first bad check back was the $600 check, which Mr. Able had cashed. It had been drawn on a New York bank and got back to us in five days, about par for the course, and there was the familiar refrain, "Signature illegible, account unknown." However, the $1,100 check still hadn't bounced and so, being exceedingly polite, we simply charged the $600 check against the savings account, leaving a balance of $980. But the next day the bottom fell out, because chugging back from California, thirteen days (or three days longer than usual) after it had been deposited, came the tattered $1,100, returned with the notation "Unable to locate account." To complete the cycle, the $475 check Mr. Able deposited on the day he cashed the $600 check came floating back a couple of days later. When the tumult and the shouting were over, First Mutual Trust Company was out a fast $595. (The $600 bad check, minus the $5 left from the original $25 deposit.)

The lessons here are fairly obvious: any time a customer walks in and he is a transient, treat the matter gingerly. Mr. Able's transaction smelled from the minute it opened. The teller who allowed him to take $20 out of his original $25 deposit should have made a note. Somebody in operations at Mr. Able's branch should have spotted the irregularity of a $1,100 deposit, made at a different branch, to an account which had been opened with $25. The teller who cashed the $600 check violated a cardinal rule of the bank: no teller is allowed to cash a check for over $500 without sending to the platform for approval. (The teller had been with us for twenty-three years and she said she was sorry.) The officer who opened the account is just as culpable, if not more so. Officers are good guys, clean, honest, well spoken, and supposedly their heads are filled with a modicum of sense. The officer took the $25 in cash to open the account and from May to July did nothing to check the background of the customer. You can't say, "We don't want your account," but you certainly can open the account and then take some action.

I said earlier that last year our "accounts receivable" on frauds ran to roughly $600,000. As an average, let's say that each transaction cost us $100. Roughly speaking, then, we're talking about 6,000 stupid transactions a year. There are approximately 250 working days in a given year; therefore I can look at the trusted employees of First Mutual Trust and say that every day, in one of our 126 branches, our employees allow more than twenty truly hair-raising transactions to take place.

The astute reader will have perceived that Mr. Able's swindle couldn't have taken place had there not been a delay while his bum $1,100 check rode a slow stagecoach to California and back, taking from July 13 to July 25. Granted, the $1,100 was an interbranch deposit, so call it from July 14 to the 25th, which still is eleven days. Had that check gone out to California and back in five or six days, the scheme would have collapsed.

The basic problem is that the banking industry has so successfully convinced the American public to write checks that we now write about 23 billion checks a year. This can be interpreted to mean a lot of things, but what it boils down to is one hell of a lot of paperwork. The Federal Reserve Banking System, which is comprised of twelve district banks around the country plus twenty-four branches, has suddenly awakened to the fact that commercial banks throughout the country have been quietly ripping off the federal system for years.

Because the Federal Reserve bank extends credit to commercial banks, most if not all banks have taken the Fed for millions of dollars each year. It works this way. If you buy a suit of clothes at a store on Times Square using your Hoboken bank's check, the clothing store, not wanting to hold on to your check for more than twenty minutes, deposits it immediately to its own New York bank. In turn, the New York bank ships it right off to the Federal Reserve Bank in New York, where it (the New York bank) is immediately given credit by the Federal Reserve System for your check. It might take the Fed two or three days before it collects on your check; all the while it is losing potential interest on that $79.95 suit of yours.

In 1971, as I said, we wrote 23 billion checks, which is a figure that is increasing about 7 percent a year and is expected to reach 44 billion checks in 1980. It has been calculated that on any given day the Federal Reserve System is extending about $3 billion in credit. Given the fact that the Fed could get 5 percent interest on this $3 billion, it works out to about $150 million a day that it is losing because of the "float," which is the nondescriptive phrase given to this polite form of banking check kiting.

In 1971 the Federal Reserve System took a look at this merry-go-round of floating checks and decided to try to put an end to it. They've instituted a new program which they hope will get some efficiency into the entire check-clearing process. If the Fed succeeds, the reform will affect giant companies which try to keep as little cash as they can in the bank not earning interest for them; cities like New York which, because of the float, earn a considerable amount of interest each year by writing checks and calculating that they won't have to cover them for five or six days; and plain ordinary deadbeats, like you and me, who write checks and then worry about covering them four days later. And, of course, swindlers who have traditionally counted on the dilapidated check-recovery system of this country to support their activities.

The Fed's overhaul of check clearing is supposed to start taking effect in a few months, and I wish them well. What the Federal Reserve System is really shooting for is to eliminate much of the nation's checkwriting by 1980 and to convert the country to an electronic payment system — the so-called checkless society. In this scheme of things, your paycheck will automatically be transferred to your bank's computer. Theoretically, many of the nation's stores will be on a true credit card system, all hooked into a central computer network. In this magical world of no money, the customer will never have to sully his hands.

In my opinion it might happen, but I think this wonderful era of banking is far in the future — much farther than the Fed realizes. First of all, the nation's banks have done quite a marvelous job in convincing people to write checks; it will not be that easy to take away those puce checkbooks from all of those happy checkwriting customers. And secondly, to cure the nation's float, much less to get the entire country on a checkless system, we will have to work the bugs out of all our computer installations. That there are bugs is all too obvious to the banking public; I can't begin to enumerate the complaints we have to handle as a result of faulty computer programming or operational printouts. And finally, the banks of this country are facing a personnel crisis of stupendous proportions; the nonmanagement turnover keeps rising and the quality of clerical help is falling. You can't run any kind of system, much less a computer-based checkless system, without the technical and operational people to back it up.

Although the Fed thinks that the day will come when retailers will simply send our bills to the bank where a computer will deduct the amount from our account, the straws which have been cast to the wind so far have not been encouraging. The Federal Reserve Bank of Atlanta did a survey recently in which it discovered that bank customers did not cotton to the idea. Closer to home, the Franklin National Bank of New York went out and hired a market research firm to test the notion of automatic bill paying among its customers and Franklin National's customers did not like the concept either.

Although banking theoreticians envision smoothly running computers eliminating the blizzard of checks we now have, nobody has thought of overhauling the dependency we place today on the canceled check. From fighting the Internal Revenue Service to fighting your landlord, the canceled check is, in today's litigious world, a necessity, not a luxury. Internal Revenue can examine your returns after they're three years old, and woe to the man who can't produce his canceled checks. So while the Federal Reserve and banking authorities may promote the new checkless society, it is my opinion that society itself is going to have to undergo basic structural changes before this brave new computer world can be born.

And as hard as the Fed is going to try and eliminate checks, they'll never get rid of the free spirit of swindlers: the most colorful band I ever heard of was a gang which methodically went around and stole complete sets of firemen's uniforms — badges, axes, hats, paychecks, everything but the hook and ladder. Once they had an official paycheck in hand, they immediately started printing their own. Four or five members of the ring would stroll into a branch, brandishing their gear, show their phony badges for identification, and cash a bad check. We got hit for $8,000, but other banks in the New York area were taken for much more. The total ran to about $100,000. And the banks, what did we do? Naturally, we issued an interbank memo which said in effect be on the lookout for firemen cashing paychecks. I daresay they'll turn up as policemen next.

# CHAPTER III

FIRST Mutual Trust Company, which is the parent holding company for First Mutual Trust Bank, has approximately 10,000 employees, and of those 10,000 roughly 2,000 are officers. Now I am objective, but no matter how I look at that figure of 2,000 my blood chills. One officer for every four employees is an unbelievable number of officers, and it is the best example I can think of Parkinson's Law and the Peter Principle, except that it's in dead earnest.

It used to be a joke that advertising agencies were afflicted with vice presidents — instead of a raise a man got a title. This same process is at work in banks, only infinitely more so. We have one vice president who is in charge of ordering water carafes. This is the *reductio ad absurdum* but it is true. We have more paper- and pencil-pushers than Dr. Parkinson or Dr. Peter could ever imagine in their wildest dreams.

In a nation which prides itself on efficiency, management experts, and time and motion studies, we have two thousand officers. Our ratio, I should imagine, is about the same as it is in any large U.S. bank. Nobody knows for sure how the officer corps grew to the size that it did or to the absurdity that it did; one can only guess. Banks traditionally have been privately owned, or at least the bulk of their voting stock has been closely held by one family, and bankers who own their own banks are nothing but human: they don't like to pay the troops. You can take the banker out of the moneylender category but you can't take the moneylender out of the banker. It is my uneducated guess that as the banks grew and as the peons proliferated, the owners of the banks were faced with (as they call such things in the business schools) options: (1) either pay the peons more or (2) give them a title. I have been an officer for nigh on to fifteen years and I still don't know what half of the officers in our bank actually do.

One thing they do is they get to work on time. A very big thing, getting to work on time: none of your excuses about the New Haven railroad not working, a subway fire. In by 9 A.M., out by 5 P.M. This we all do, two thousand of us, every day of the year. Well, almost every day of the year, but vacation plans come a little later.

To cope with the two thousand of us is no little task: we have an enormous personnel operation which does nothing but move names up the charts, sideways on the charts, and rarely off the charts. We went through a bit of a crisis a couple of years ago when one of the chief officers of the personnel operation, Lance, was married, but suspiciously so. Indeed, a friend of mine once saw Lance cruising Third Avenue during a Long Island Railroad strike, when he couldn't get home to the wife and kids, and he was not looking for girls. I suppose one might say that he was out scouting for potential vice presidents of the bank. One could say that but I won't. However, he was so zealous in his recruiting that for a while we were inundated by a pack of staggeringly handsome executives who compared tans more than they compared golf scores. And while golf scores are *de rigueur* in a bank, tans aren't, and eventually the *caballero* from personnel was sent away.

At some point in our bank a genius sat down and devised a system for keeping track of all of us. He wrote the Officers Handbook, a 300-page thriller that tells us just about everything we need to know about conducting our business life with the exception of going to the bathroom. (I do not want to stoop to lavatory humor in my discussion of bank officers, but I do feel it is worth mentioning that one of the officers in our bank — an officer who is concerned with the handling of money — is a germ freak. When he goes to the bathroom, he very carefully takes two tissues and gingerly relieves himself. His organ is untouched by human hands, as it were. I mention this only because I assume he has the same germlike aversion to the handling of money as well. Needless to say, he also has a set of crazy nasal filters for venturing outside of the bank. His behavior, I might add, is widely known at the bank and it has not hampered his career in the slightest. He does use up a lot of tissue, though.)

The entire officer corps, from the newest and the lowest to the chairman of the board, is geared to a grading system, not unlike the GS system used in the government to classify civil servants.

We, as do most banks, have the title of "assistant treasurer," a very enigmatic description and nomenclature. To outsiders, assistant treasurer implies one step below the treasurer, and since banks are money, the treasurer must really have his power. When I joined First Mutual and became an assistant treasurer, my mother introduced me to her friends as "my son the assistant treasurer," and the entire neighborhood of Nutley, New Jersey, was stunned with my importance. What my mother did not tell her neighbors, since she didn't know the truth, and what I didn't tell my mother, since I was too embarrassed, was that First Mutual had roughly a thousand assistant treasurers, all of whom were scrambling up the promotional ladder and none of whom worked for *the* treasurer because we don't have a treasurer.

In our bank we have a numerical rating scale that for officers starts at 30 (the newest assistant treasurer) and ends at 52 (the chairman of the board). There are three grades of assistant treasurers at our bank, with the corresponding numerical rankings of 30, 32, and 34. The salary range for an assistant treasurer is from $10,000 to $15,000 a year; the $10,000 salary equivalent to 30, $12,500 matching 32 and $15,000 comparable to 34.

Naturally we believe that this system is equitable and fair. Of course it isn't. There are assistant treasurers and then there are assistant treasurers who are going to be moving up the ladder in a hurry. Those in a hurry breeze into the bank with a gold-plated introduction from their father or their Uncle Harry, who happens to have $2 million in the hands of our trust department. They go through our executive training program and then might be put into the trust department where they'll go to work at $14,000 or $15,-000 a year. Within five or six years these officers will be full-fledged vice presidents.

But because we guarantee equality to all, a trusted employee of ours might have laboriously worked his way up from teller, to the platform, to an assistant managership, and finally one day his ship will come in: he will be asked to become an officer of First Mutual Trust Company. He will be allowed to get up at 6:30 A.M. so he can get down to the main vault at 8:30 A.M. and help open that gigantic thing once a year; and he will have all the other perks of an officer. He'll be an assistant treasurer, too, but since he doesn't have an Uncle Harry, he'll become an officer at $11,000 a year or so. The irony of it is that he'll be placed in a retail branch as a manager, with direct responsibility of the safe passage of hundreds of thousands of dollars a year in very liquid funds.

The gold-plated officer who is quietly buried in the trust department has no more responsibility than keeping his clients, who usually are old but very rich ladies, happy. If he keeps his nails clean he will become a vice president, and once you're a vice president they don't remove you from office.

But the inherent trap in the rating system is that those officers not destined to greatness but rather destined to run branch offices in Brooklyn for the rest of their lives cannot escape the rating system. The tradition in the bank is that if you're not promoted up by the time you hit the middle of your rating, you never will be. Therefore, the assistant treasurer who comes in with a ranking of 30 and a salary of $10,000 and who receives increases to $12,500 must be made an assistant vice president after a couple of years. If he simply is given more money, let's say to $14,000, he rises to the top numerical ranking in the category, 30, and he will never go beyond it. Never. Which is why assistant treasurers sometimes get involved in schemes which end up losing the bank lots of money.

All promotions must go through the board of directors, and if you're promoted, it takes place on the third Wednesday of every month except for July and August — the two

months that the board of directors have better things to oc-
cupy themselves with than promoting assistant treasurers. A
strange air comes over the bank on Promotion Wednesday:
the lower echelon wears blue suits and white shirts. At ten
of five, your immediate superior's secretary calls you in and
your superior usually gives you a touching little speech
about you and First Mutual Trust. For the man who has
been working in the bank all his life, having started as a
teller or a clerk, and has been asked to join the priesthood,
the promotion to the officer ranks is overwhelming. Grown
men in their forties or fifties have been known to break
down and cry with emotion. Younger employees tend to be
a little more blasé about it, reflecting the gradual change in
spirit at the bank.

At the very top of the heap — the pope, as it were —
stands the chairman of the board, which is a long way
from assistant treasurerhood. His salary at First Mutual
Trust is over $200,000, which is fairly good as chairmen of
the board of banks go. His salary is not a secret — it's
published in the annual report of the bank to its
stockholders — but he still is a bit touchy about it. At the
annual meeting of the officers of the bank, one assistant
vice president, obviously overcome with ambition and alco-
hol, stood up and asked the chairman point-blank what his
salary was. This dinner is of a ceremonial nature, and although there is a question-and-answer period, one doesn't
go around asking the chairman if he has enough salary to
pay his bills. The chairman handled the Nosey Parker with
what I felt was considerable aplomb, "Look it up in the annual report." Which we all did.

The assistant vice president range on the scale runs from

36 to 38; the comparable salaries are much more flexible
and run from $17,000 to $23,000. Here again, the crucial
thing is not if you reach the 38-point level as an assistant
vice president, but rather if you're moved out of the assistant
vice presidential range up to the vice presidency.

A vice presidency in a bank is the promised land: once
there, they can't send you away from the fiscal land of milk
and honey. It isn't that a vice president makes such a great
sum of money — the salary range is from $24,000 to
$45,000. But, much more important, it is another way of
life. Work slows down, lunches lengthen perceptibly, opin-
ions are listened to more carefully, responsibility grows or
absolutely vanishes, depending on the individual's inclination for work. Although the ratings for a vice president run
from 40 to 44, they really don't tell the whole story.

There are vice presidents and then there are vice presidents. A vice president rarely runs a retail branch, i.e., the
rank is much too high for the job. However, we have two
or three vice presidents in charge of our large commercial
branches: on Fifth Avenue, on Seventh Avenue in the garment center, and down in Wall Street. These are run by full
vice presidents, and they would be paid at the higher end of
the scale. After all, they're managing large businesses; they
have loan approval of $250,000 and beyond; and their re-
sponsibility at times is much larger than our chairman's.

Our chairman's main function is to look like a chairman.
In the winter he's gone every Thursday for Palm Springs, in
the summer, Southampton. Nobody begrudges him his
jaunts: we regard them as business, not pleasure. As long as
his banker's-gray hair holds out, he's more than welcome to
represent us at the best watering holes he can find. God

help him, though, if he develops dandruff or starts going bald. Then he's going to have to go out and find himself a job.

A vice president who has risen through the ranks on the operational side and works in deposit accounting, check processing, or computer operations, and essentially is hidden from public view, is paid $27,000 to $30,000. A trust vice president who has to have clean breath, capped teeth, and a way with women is worth more to us — say $35,000 a year. And then there is time off. The vacation schedule for a bank vice president is absolutely dynamite. You've got six weeks' vacation as a vice president (as opposed to only four weeks as an assistant vice president) and that's not six work weeks, that's one full month plus fourteen days off.

Assuming that there are 52 weeks in a year and 5 work days to a week, there are, in a bank officer's life, roughly 260 work days to contend with. Subtract from that one month (30 days) and two weeks (14 days) and you're left with 214 work days. A vice president celebrates 11, count 'em, 11 holidays a year, which brings us down to 203 work days, and you're given 8 days to take as "sick days" even though you can get sick for a hell of a lot longer and not have it deducted. Two hundred and three work days less 8 "sick days" brings us down to about 195 days of actual hard work. If you want to divide 195 by 5 days to a given week you'll end up with less than 40 weeks a year.* I have yet to get into two-hour lunches, which are par for the course of a vice president, nor have I touched on the national sport of banking, golf, which in the spring and summer manages to cut into quiet afternoons. And I haven't

* If you enjoy balancing your checkbook, feel free to audit these figures. Even a banker can make mistakes.

discussed banking conventions, or special conferences, or seminars away from home, or just plain muddleheaded day-dreaming about the prime rate. In this day of talk about four-day work weeks, in this day of boasting by unions about their terrific new contracts, in this day of three-day holiday weekends sanctioned by the government, in this time of expanded leisure and recreation, just remember one thing, friends: your banker was there way ahead of you.

You may think you know all about time off; forget it. Bankers have done more creative work in this area than officers in any other industry going today, and that dopey look on his face when you complain about your account comes from his distaste of trying to figure out how the computer bollixed up your deposits. All he wants to do is worry about his boat, his golf game, his airplane, his time off. On the job with body, but not soul.

Beyond vice president, the air gets a bit rarefied as the rating system works toward 52. Senior vice presidents come next up the ladder, then first vice presidents, executive vice presidents, the president, vice chairman of the board, and then the chairman. The vice presidential range on the scale runs from 40 through 46 because it covers the various permutations. The president is 48, the vice chairman is 50, and then bingo! The salaries begin to loosen up considerably as soon as you get into the senior, first, and executive vice president range, and they run from the $50,000 level at the low end on up.

All of us are in a complicated stock/profit-sharing program — we contribute so much, the bank kicks in its share, and you end up with so many shares of First Mutual Trust Company stock. We have extremely good major medical and health insurance programs. We are plugged into a retirement program. We are indeed a way of life. On top of all this most major banks have a very nice line of credit set up for their officers. At our bank a vice president has an automatic line of credit of $10,000, usually obtainable at one half of whatever rate the bank is lending money out at that given time. If the loan rate to regular customers is 7½ percent, we can borrow up to our loan limit at 3¾ percent. Our handbook says point-blank that these loans are not to be used for speculative ventures, but rather for boats, cars, home repairs — or exactly the same criteria we use when we lend money to the man off the street. However, who knows how many of these officers' loans are funneled into a hot stock? I don't know, but I can guess that quite a bit of them are. As with salaries, the line of credit goes up with rank.

The assistant treasurers and the assistant vice presidents really work like dogs in a bank because they see what's ahead of them. Most vice presidents have at least an assistant treasurer and usually an assistant vice president working for them, the assistants slaving away because *they* want to be promoted to a softer job. If none of the above inducements are reason enough for staying in a bank, an ambitious employee has one final reason: banks tend to pay their chief executive officers *very* well. In 1971, many of the country's top bankers managed to give themselves a nice raise despite a drop in profits by most banks. W. B. Wriston, chairman of the First National City Corporation, did not get a raise: his salary remained at the 1970 figure — $275,820. David Rockefeller, chairman of Chase Manhattan, took a salary cut: in 1970 he was paid $264,500, but in 1971 he sank to $263,926. I have visions of Mr. Rockefeller coming home the night he learned that his salary dropped $574 and insisting on chuck for dinner, rather than ground round. Hard times at the Rockefeller table. Most of the chairmen of the New York, Chicago, and West Coast banking giants manage pretty well. Gabriel Hauge, chairman of Manufacturers Hanover, is paid $218,375; W. S. Renchard, chairman of Chemical New York, is paid $230,304; W. H. Moore, chairman of Bankers Trust New York, a rounded-off $233,200; G. A. Freeman, Jr., chairman of First Chicago Corporation, is paid a nifty $248,-600; and R. P. Cooley, head of Wells Fargo out in San Francisco, manages to get by on $224,836.

I sometimes get a little wistful when I look at all of the salaries soaring above $200,000 a year and I realize that the chairman of First Mutual Trust Company is not too high on the list. But I am able to take consolation in the fact that our chairman probably works less at his job than any other chairman of any other major bank in the United States. I was not casually kidding about his being a showpiece: it has been suggested more than once at First Mutual Trust that we ought to stuff our chairman and hang him at the entrance of our main branch.

One word pervades all talk about what it's like to be an officer in the bank: the word is comfortable. If you've been with the bank for a couple of years as an officer and you're promoted up to the next grade, you know that you have a certain amount of ability and that if you stay out of trouble and out of the newspapers you'll move up from assistant treasurer to assistant vice president, and in another three years if your luck holds and you function well you'll move up to the first rung of vice presidents. The reason we have so many officers who don't move at all is because at some point in their career they suddenly go lazy.

Since much of your advancement depends on your immediate supervisor's appraisal of you, the law of averages says that eventually you'll hit a bastard; it is at this point where people get lazy and work just hard enough to keep their immediate supervisor content. They organize their jobs so that they don't have to do too much work, and when you ask someone who has not moved up in grade why he stays, he says, "Well, they're not paying me that much by industry standards, but when you look at it on an hourly basis it's quite a nice salary and I'm very comfortable. In other words, Big Brother, or in this case Mother Bank, is watching out for you. It's a comfortable life and you're respected in your community.

Among the lower and middle range of bank officers, your personnel file and appraisal are all-important; you are promoted or kept in place solely on the appraisals. A full appraisal must be written every three years; during the interim it is kept up-to-date with footnotes, addenda, and so forth. The top part of the appraisal is a job description and then a written report on how you perform in that specified job. Are you in or out of the conventional guidelines of the job, parameterwise? Your superior rates your efficiency and points out where you are doing well, fair, or poorly, and where you need improvement and what steps are being taken to improve your poor performance. Finally, does your superior officer recommend you for advancement? This appraisal is kept on file with personnel and is so much like the military officer's form that the resemblance is frightening.

Obviously, this system has all of the dubious faults of the military system for evaluating personnel. If you have committed the banking equivalent of My Lai — let's say you proposed the building of a new branch which was promptly burned down by hostile natives — your superior officer can cover up or not; it simply depends on how he feels about you personally. Conversely, if you have managed to save the bank $400,000 by instituting a new computer program which rounds off decimals in the bank's favor, you won't go up life's ladder unless your boss likes you.

The free enterprise system is something that banks are forever trumpeting about; they don't practice it in their own ranks. Let us say I work for First Mutual Trust Company and I have a chat with an officer at Chase and I suggest that I could do great things for Chase. The man from Chase might even imply that there's always a niche at Chase if I want it. I cannot go back to First Mutual Trust and use Chase's interest to further my career at First Mutual. That is strictly verboten at our bank and usually at every bank in the U.S. That is, I as a vice president can't waltz into my boss and say, "Chase wants me and they're offering me X dollars more a year, and what is First Mutual Trust going to do about this?" "Nothing" is First Mutual's answer. Nobody pushes us into a promotion — or even a raise, for that matter.

In banking, more than in almost any other industry, there is a very rigid Old Boys' network, and if someone decides to try and upset the network, the network jumps down hard on the offender. There is very little switching from one bank to another by bank officers. On the lower and middle officer level, a bank which is being solicited by the officer would immediately check with the officer's own bank. If I want to go to work for Chase I have to leave First Mutual and then begin to look for a job at Chase. But if I were to bounce into Chase and say, "Please keep this

under your hat, First Mutual doesn't know that I'm looking," the odds are that someone at Chase would talk to
someone at First Mutual Trust. We are typical and not a little vindictive. Our personnel department would tell Chase
that Morgan Irving is fine, when he gets that little drinking
problem under control, and oh, by the way, we did have a
little problem of his misquoting interest rates on a $10 mil-
lion bond offer. Otherwise, he's tops. Chase will back
away, but what's even worse, First Mutual will have a
lovely black mark to put into its file on me.

For these reasons you don't see too much interbank
movement. When a bank goes outside its ranks, it's usually
for the president's job or perhaps the chairman's. Then the
outsider is a star — either in politics, or international economics, or diplomacy. Even then, banks are usually quite
careful when they name such a person. For the bank's
board of directors knows that the reason they have 10,000
people and 2,000 officers toeing the mark is because everyone believes he has a chance to move up one step. If a bank
goes outside too often, rumbling in the ranks occurs. The
system is built around the concept that the lowliest gun car-
rier in the most distant branch has a chance at becoming
president. Of course there is no reality to such an attitude;
but then money has very little reality itself.

So far I've only discussed successes. Promotions, salaries,
raises, and so forth. There are failures in banks, but we are
very much like the Catholic church (at least like the
Church until recently) — we don't let the failures loose. If
the church has a problem with a priest who's been nipping
at the sacramental wine a little too lovingly, then the
church has a nice, tidy, verdant home for boozing priests to
dry out. We do get rid of officers with sticky fingers; embez-

zling is a combination of twelve mortal sins in a bank. But for pure and simple fuckups — and there is no elegant way to describe them — banks have their own charitable system.

If an officer just burns out and he is in the international division of the bank, he'll be transferred out of any position of responsibility and assigned to an area where his decisions can't harm either himself or the bank. The officer who was handling sensitive transactions for the Vatican in Rome (and we have a sizable amount of business from the Church — in Rome and in New York) might be quietly handed some accounts in Madrid, which is small, quaint, and does next to nothing in the way of business. And the brandy is cheap.

It is not difficult to take care of a wrongo in the national division. The banker slightly over the hill in the group handling accounts in, say, San Francisco, might be reassigned to a region that includes a city like Louisville. Nobody does much banking in Louisville, especially First Mutual Trust Company. For those officers in the trust department whose teeth won't take any more caps and whose breath is beginning to bother the rich clients, the answer is not a better mouthwash but a different desk in the bank.

It's not so easy when the officer in question has problems beyond a question of competency. One of our officers was moving surefootedly to the top of the heap when it was discovered that he was a full-fledged pyromaniac. In a bank this can be a dangerous thing; after all, money is paper. Although we're geared to handle sex perverts, embezzlers, and freaks of one stripe or another, the pyromaniac caused real consternation.

Obviously, he had been a pyromaniac for a long time.

He used to have an office at our main location uptown, and one day it was discovered that the curtains in his office were singed. The incident was blamed on indolent workmen fiddling with the wiring in the building and nothing was thought of the matter. A couple of years later the same thing happened, singed curtains. I don't know what the official explanation was, but the incident was not put together with the first, and he went on his upward way. Finally, this officer showed up at a Christmas party and got drunk. He sat in the corner of the restaurant singing carols and started throwing lit matches at the Christmas tree. Nobody wants to be in a fire, and bank officers are not much different from your run-of-the-mill citizen in this respect, so the pyromaniac was finally told to cut it out, for God's sake. He sulked in the corner for an hour or so and we all forgot about it. Suddenly one of the secretaries started to scream, and when we all turned around the Christmas tree was blazing away and the officer who had been sulking was grinning as if the prime rate had just gone up two percentage points.

After the fire department quieted things down a couple of people remembered that the officer had had some suspicious goings-on with burned curtains and he was confronted with these facts. He denied them. He had always been loyal to First Mutual Trust Company and we do reward loyalty, in our fashion. He ended his career as the manager of a remote (but fireproof) branch out on Long Island, which did not have a single curtain.

Like every other business enterprise, we have our share of breakups, breakdowns, people flipping out right on the banking floor, officers going slightly balmy at the sight of all the money lying around loose. The saddest nervous breakdown that I can recall happened to a forty-year-old assistant treasurer who had been running a branch out in Brooklyn. He was not one of our high flyers; he was not preordained to be one of our stars. He hadn't gone to college; rather, he had worked his way up through the ranks and had finally reached his Camelot — assistant treasurer. He fell in love with one of the tellers in the branch and they decided to get married. Further, they wanted to buy a little house in Levittown — they even had it picked out. To finance the house he had to take his savings out of a deferred income program, which we run for all the employees. The rules state that when you put money into this program you can't touch it until you retire or if you give the bank two years' notice. If you insist on drawing the money out in an emergency, you can do it, but you are penalized a small sum. The bank, however, refused to give him his money, saying that it would set a bad example for other employees. He had already married and the little house had become an obsession with him. The bank couldn't have cared less. Every day he would call the personnel office and beg for his money and every day the personnel office would cite whatever chapter and verse of the rules were applicable. This went on for three months until one day he simply cracked on the job and went berserk. They had to haul him away and he was hospitalized for several months. The ironical thing about it was that the bank and its insurance company had to pay a hell of a stiff bill in medical coverage because of his breakdown. When he returned to work, they sent him to the bank's equivalent of Siberia, a floating branch manager status, which is a little like being a permanent substitute schoolteacher in a large school system.

We call our Siberia "branch rotation assignment," and it

contains a very sad group of people. These are officers on the middle to lower-middle level who just didn't work out for one reason or another: perhaps they drank, perhaps there was a personality conflict. Usually, these officers are in their mid-fifties: they can't go any further because the system has said that they have gone as far as they will go. The bank, however, in its infinite mercy, has decreed that they will be pensioned off and sent to live out their golden years in bitterness. They become floating managers, and ever week, on Friday, they call in to headquarters and find out where they'll be working the next week. Perhaps a branch manager in Astoria has the flu; Astoria it is. Maybe a new branch is being opened and a few more presentable bodies are needed to handle the first-day crowds. Essentially, the floating managers fill in when the permanent managers go on vacation.

This is Siberia on the lower level. On the middle level, assistant vice president and vice president, the bank still tries to protect its own. Officers who had been receiving promotions and raises steadily for twenty years or so might suddenly find that their upward progress has stopped. Two, three, or perhaps four years might pass without a glimmer of a promotion and then the bank decides to do something with the officer. One officer I know found himself called the "vault officer"; that is, the officer in charge of vaults. It is a meaningless job and an even less meaningful title. The bank has literally dozens of jobs which require very little work or intelligence. We have quite a large coin and currency department, whose function it is to count and wrap coins and currency. Coin and currency is a fine spot to put an officer whose reflexes have dulled.

Naturally, a department as mundane as coin and currency is always popping up with a strange scandal. A few years ago it was discovered that our coin and currency people were busily manufacturing phony subway tokens at home — a neat cottage industry — and then slyly selling them to bank customers as the real thing. Evidently one of the employees in the department had got his hands on a coin-manufacturing machine. Since our bank, like many New York banks, sells tokens to customers, the customers don't look over each token they buy from the bank to see if it's a slug.

Eventually, the bad tokens worked their way into the New York City transit system, and sure enough, they were traced back to us. Five people were fired and among the five was one officer of the bank.

When an officer leaves the bank under circumstances less than normal — that is, when he is either fired or asked to leave — it usually is done as quietly as possible. In most cases, a small lunch will be arranged for the officer's last day of work, usually attended by only one or two other officers. The lunches are always awkward and it is hard to figure who is the most embarrassed by them — the officer leaving or the two officers who are staying.

If one of our officers is told that he ought to look around for another job, the bank normally gives him several months to relocate himself. If we're letting him go simply because he's stupid or inefficient, we might even help relocate him. A classic case of this sort took place in our trust department when one of the officers was just hopeless. However, he hadn't embezzled or raped or pillaged, so when this officer went job hunting and the personnel department of a potential employer checked back with our personnel people, we decided not to hinder the man's ca-

reer. We didn't say that the officer was one of God's stupid-
est creations, we simply chalked up his desire to leave our
bosom to "personality conflict," which covers a multitude
of sins. And, in this officer's favor, he had done a good job
on selling himself to the new people — he also used the
personality conflict story. He got the job and when it came
time for him to depart First Mutual Trust Company's
shores, someone decided to give him a bangup farewell
luncheon.

It was a disaster. The junior officer who arranged the
luncheon did not realize that the officer was leaving because he was not wanted. The younger man simply thought
his superior had gone on to even greater glory. In arranging
the luncheon, he managed to coerce about twenty officers
to attend, and few if any of them thought that there were
going to be more than one or two officers at the luncheon.
The junior officer bought a gift, and arranged the luncheon
at a private club in the city. Imagine the look on everyone's
face — including the man leaving — when twenty-one officers assembled for a lunch that none of them wanted to attend. The luncheon dragged on like an execution, and even
the small talk tailed off into huge, empty silences. Finally,
the senior officer attending the lunch stood up, mumbled a
few words, and handed the gift to the departing officer. The
officer leaving stood up and said simply that he thought
First Mutual Trust Company was a snakepit, and as far as
he was concerned, he hoped that it went down the drain,
the sooner the better. He left the gift, turned, and walked
out of the lunch. It took the group about fifteen minutes to
recover.

Occasionally, there are officers that the bank doesn't
know how to get rid of. One of these is a former vice presi-

dent named Ralph, who is in his fifties. The bank has asked
him several times to retire, and each time Ralph has told
the bank that he doesn't want to stay home with his wife
and he won't quit. At one time he was one of the most
powerful men in the bank. Unfortunately, he took to the
bottle, as they say, and he became a fairly nasty and incompetent drunk. During the 1950s and 1960s, when every
bank in New York was expanding all over the lot, we were
standing still because of Ralph, who lived for the good old
days and refused to modernize our systems. He had a
trusted secretary, and as he became more of a drunk the
secretary actually took over more and more of his func-
tions. He played favorites, he fired people for no reason
whatsoever, he ruined careers, and he broke people on a
whim. When the ruling hierarchy of the bank finally caught
up with him and decided that this just couldn't go on, he
had come very close to ruining the bank's future.

But he won't leave, and in a way we don't want him to
leave. The chances are that he could easily walk over to
Chemical, or Chase, or one of the leading banks and offer
his services. Despite his drinking, he still knows quite a bit
about our day-to-day operation, and his status is quite akin
to a burned-out spy. Although he's outlived his usefulness
to us, we sure don't want him traipsing over to the Rus-
sians. This, of course, makes a considerable presumption
on our part: that the systems of ours with which he is so familiar would indeed be valuable to another bank. About
this, I'm not so sure. Much of our bank is so haphazardly
run that I have often felt that perhaps it would be to our
advantage to ship Ralph to Chase, First National, Chemical, or Bankers Trust. Let him foul their nest, not ours.

A couple of years ago the chairman and the president

decided to cut what they considered to be deadwood from the officer corps; this was the first time in the memory of the bank when trusted and loyal employees were given the heave-ho without allowing them to lounge around the bank gracefully until they were due to retire. The reason given for the firing was "the deadwood syndrome," but the real reason was that the bank was not doing well at all. During the years 1969, 1970, and 1971, all banks in New York were having their problems. Interest rates had soared, customers were putting their money into their savings accounts and leaving it there, and the banks, reflecting the rest of the Nixon economy, were in trouble. First Mutual Trust was no exception. When in trouble, fire, because it's money in the bank, to coin a phrase.

Since we had approximately 10,000 employees, an arbitrary percentage of 6 percent was fixed as the number of people who had to go. That's roughly 600 employees, and if you calculate that the median salary plus benefits to carry those 600 employees was $10,000 a person, then on your balance sheet you're picking up about $6,000,000 of sheer profit for the next year. This is an easy way to boost the earnings per share of any company; even a bank knows that. Of the 600, about 100 of these were officers — many of them old-timers who believed in the right and the goodness of First Mutual Trust and who truly had devoted their entire working lives to the bank. The line of reasoning went like this: We've got to become competitive with industry and banks are no longer going to be places where people just find a job and stay.

The firings were preceded by an immense amount of list-making — who goes and who stays. Secret lists were denied. The sadness of it was that officers who knew they weren't particularly bright always felt that they had a place at First Mutual Trust Company.

A majority of the officers were in their late fifties or early sixties, and although I will grant that many of those let go or "retired early" were not first-rate, the premise of the bank had always been to hire and then nurture mediocrity.

As with many of the projects that First Mutual gets into, the mass firings were handled badly. You really can't fire 600 people — and especially 100 officers — without managing to alert the rest of the business community to what you've been up to. And when any company — Boeing in Seattle is a pretty good example — starts laying off people by the hundreds, the toll in bad public relations is horrendous. Nobody at First Mutual had considered the public relations aspect of the firings: they only had eyes for the $6,-000,000 they were going to save.

Where they really ran into trouble were with the three senior vice presidents they were planning to fire. A senior vice president in a New York City bank has been around and he usually knows people on the *Times,* or *Barron's,* or on the *Wall Street Journal.* The three senior vice presidents were, let's say, named Smith, Jones, and Brown, and the president of the bank went to them and said, "This is it. Early retirement." Only the president didn't really know what he was dealing with.

All three of the senior vice presidents politely but firmly told the president that they weren't leaving — unless, that is, First Mutual wanted the details of the firings spread all over the daily newspapers and the banking media. As far as I can gather, this was an unprecedented revolt by an officer. The president was first stunned, second mad as hell, and finally nonplussed; he didn't know what to do. He knew full well that between them, Smith, Jones, and Brown had enough clout to do what they threatened to do. And already the media had been calling the beleaguered public relations department of the bank asking about the rumors of the firings that were going on.

The bank was blithely denying that any firing was going on. Ironically, all of this was taking place in the early part of February, and sure enough, some of the more embittered were calling it the St. Valentine's Day Massacre. Nobody at the top was terribly concerned about the 500 in clerical help. The attitude was, what the hell, they'll find another job without any difficulty. And the bank had very little feeling about letting officers go who had served the bank for thirty or forty years. The bank only was worried when it appeared that the three big guns, Smith, Jones, and Brown, were going to create havoc.

Meanwhile, the press was increasing pressure on the public relations people for an answer to what was really going on. The anonymous First Mutual Trust Company spokesmen who spoke for the bank talked vaguely of early retirement for some who had requested it; he talked about freezing hiring; he mumbled something about keeping the staff levels down to manageable proportions; he muttered about bringing the bank into managerial lines with outside industry, whatever that means.

The *Times* listened to this blather and then printed an article saying that in effect blood was running through the hallowed halls of First Mutual Trust Company, which First Mutual Trust promptly denied. While the bickering between press and public relations was going on, department, section, and region heads were going over more lists of who should stay, who should go, who should be retired to his little cabin in the Poconos.

The bank stuck to its story and said that there were no firings. The financial press stuck to its story, but the pivotal factor was the three senior vice presidents, Smith, Jones, and Brown. The chairman and the president had been trying to cope with them during the entire fracas and had not been making much headway. Indeed, the three senior men had been told bluntly that they were through, out, finished, and they could take their pension or leave it.

The line of reasoning that Smith, Jones, and Brown pursued was infinitely more clever than the bank's. They pointed out, individually and together, that the official line of the bank was that there had not been any firings. Thus, the bank had to rehire them, because if, indeed, they had been fired, the entire financial world would know. First Mutual Trust, like every other bank, produces a staggering amount of self-congratulatory annual reports, six-month reports, quarterly advisories to stockholders and the media. Smith, Jones, and Brown were always prominently listed in this avalanche of material.

Smith et al. quickly pointed out to the president that if they were fired then the three names would have to be removed from our various reports; and if the names were suddenly missing, the media would immediately know that a purge was going on.

The president grasped the wisdom of their logic and the three were kept on, but they were stripped of their responsibilities. Now what will occur is a war of nerves: the bank will do anything it can to humiliate the three. They will be shuttled around from office to office; their secretaries will be taken away from them; and they really won't have much to do. Depending on how tough-minded the officers are, they can last until they're the official retirement age and then collect their pensions. What the bank wants, of course, is for them to capitulate, to ask for early retirement, and in their cases the bank wants to set an example for other potential rebels. The bank is very nervous about rebels and this extends all the way through the ranks of the bank. (An officer who once appeared at an annual meeting of officers wearing a purple shirt was told to leave — this is the low end of the rebel scale.)

In the middle of the hysteria of the St. Valentine's Day Massacre, somebody — and nobody can figure out exactly who — approved a flyer to be sent out to all of First Mutual Trust Company's checking account customers. The flyer, mailed in the monthly statements, said that First Mutual Trust was looking for clerical personnel, secretaries, guards, summer personnel, and so forth. The bank has ordered stringent cuts, we're not replacing secretaries, and whammo! hundreds of thousands of customers get a nifty little notice saying, "Send your nephew Marvin to us, we'll take care of him for the summer."

The personnel department, already swamped with the task of firing close to 600 people and burdened with the headaches of computing early retirements, was suddenly inundated with retired cops, retired firemen, nieces of customers, nephews named Marvin, and a splendid assortment of the walking wounded of New York City. Before the flyer was sent out, the personnel department had thinned its ranks in line with the rest of the firing that was going on throughout the bank. They had let go interviewers and had not replaced people who left. When the notice went out, they were close to collapse.

The flyer is a splendid representation of how little communication there can be in a large bank. On one floor, the top officers of the bank are walking around with secret lists of people to be fired — the expendable list. On another floor somebody pushed a button and instituted a direct mail campaign to sweep the streets for potential job applicants.

The frosting on the cake was that personnel also put a slew of ads in the *New York Times* saying that First Mutual Trust was hiring, that it was nonsense about this talk of a recession — just come on in, folks, and get on board. The flyer was finally tracked down to a guy with his head in the sand in the market services division. Obviously, nobody had told market services that bodies were being tossed out daily from the executive floors.

The reason was that the entire market services division had been wiped out, but personnel had forgot to tell them.

# CHAPTER IV

LET us now praise Vito Pagano. Vito was our only Italian vice president, more specifically, he was our only Italian first vice president, and he had been with our bank for fifteen years. We are praising Vito because just the other day he left First Mutual Trust and took a job as the president of a savings bank in Brooklyn. I don't know who owns the savings bank, nor do I know the makeup of its board of directors, but I have to suspect that somewhere in that savings bank lurks the wondrous hand of an Italian. Now don't get me wrong, some of my best friends are Italians, and Jews, and Catholics. Even a few of my friends are either black or Puerto Rican, but you don't see them around First Mutual Trust Company. First Mutual Trust, at the uppermost level, is lily white, pure, and Protestant. But it's changing, and the change is almost as interesting as the current shakeup.

To generalize about other banks for a moment, it is safe to say that most of the giant New York City banks are still run by self-perpetuating cadres of white, Anglo-Saxon Protestants. There are exceptions to the rule, obviously, but if you take the trouble to examine the composition of the top-ranking officers their names all have an astonishing sameness to them. For whatever reason, historical, sociological, or illogical, banks have never been a haven for Jews, Irish, Italians, and perish the thought, blacks. Again to generalize, the Irish Catholics (at least those who didn't become bartenders or cops), seeing that the banks were essentially closed to them, went into brokerage houses. Jews had been private investment bankers in Europe for centuries before the founding of the United States. The House of Rothschild is, of course, a prime example, and its influence is still felt today, as it has been felt so long throughout Europe and Great Britain. Southern Italians (coming from an impoverished land) have rarely got into banking, and I can't say that I blame them. As for blacks and Puerto Ricans, they've been nowhere in terms of banks and everything else, but if you were to bet on the hot ethnic groups of the next decade the best bet would be the blacks and the Puerto Ricans.

First Mutual Trust Company's top level of officers also live in splendid isolation — in areas of New York City and the suburbs that haven't seen a black face in years (except for maids) or an Italian (except for garbage removal). Actually, the top twenty-five officers of the bank don't even live in New York City proper. I give you Greenwich, Connecticut, and Cos Cob, Darien, and Stamford, Connecticut. Our generals are scattered all over Westchester County — Chappaqua and Scarsdale, Armonk and Bedford Hills. Long Island is usually anathema to the elite with the exception of Locust Valley (Oh, to be in Locust Valley when the prime rate is floating!) and Garden City. Interestingly, the rising officers of the elite group are in New Jersey, and you occasionally hear them mumble something about their bus being late. Although the average New Yorker thinks all of New Jersey is a blight on the nation, our officers have found havens of decency in Montclair and Upper Montclair, Tenafly. They are embarrassed by New Jersey and as soon as their salaries or rank permit it, they get the hell out of New Jersey to either Westchester County or Connecticut. If the restless natives of Newark burned the entire city down, our officers in New Jersey would be mentally calculating insurance losses, but nothing else.

The top ten officers of the bank usually have apartments in New York City, and the chairman also has a little hideaway in Palm Springs where he can run to in the winter. But essentially, the officers who run the bank in New York don't live in New York and therein lies the irony.

As our cities have been undergoing violent and radical change so will our banks begin to undergo change. With banks, however, change is a relative thing, and surely the alteration in our makeup will lag behind. Central cities are becoming more black — and whether you're discussing the racial composition of Washington, D.C., where the blacks range from 75 to 80 percent of the population, or St. Louis, or Philadelphia, the situation is pretty much the same. What I think will happen is that the black depositors will, without knowing it, force a change on the banking structure as we know it today. Our hottest officer at the moment is a dude named Franklin (I know, I know!) Adams, who is a so-so personnel officer with us, but who has a sparkling future. The reason is simple: at least half of our clerical personnel are black and Franklin Adams is the first admission on the part of the bank that if our operating staff is black, then there ought to be black officers as well. Franklin might well end up as a first vice president with us.

In good times our personnel department has around 150 people in it; it's a complex and varied operation that oversees the recruiting of officers as well as the logistics for training them. The implicit, but never stated, motto of all of our bank's recruiting is that the die is cast the moment you join the bank. That is, for 99 percent of all the officers who join the bank their career has been neatly charted from the moment they're asked to join our ranks.

A portion of the trainees whom we recruit come from local colleges and universities: the City College system of New York, Queens College, Brooklyn College, New York University, Hofstra College, St. John's University, Rutgers. These are not what the bank regards as elite universities. The graduates of these schools might have studied education or pursued a liberal arts degree; regardless, they are marked by a fairly prominent lack of sophistication about where their careers are heading. The recruiters who work these universities are invariably graduates of them, or similar colleges. The recruiters often regard their job as a singular honor — some of the recruiters are not even from the personnel department and they hustle on their spare time. They believe in the infallibility of God, the middle class, and First Mutual Trust Company. The picture of the bank that they depict is one of strictly metropolitan flavor. They are talking to young people from the New York City area who think that a bank is simply one or two hundred branches in all five boroughs of New York. Obviously the bank is more; we are in national and international banking, trustee banking, venture capital, and many other areas. The program that these potential recruits are told about is the assistant manager training program, the gist of which is that if they successfully complete their training, they will become the assistant manager of a branch of the bank with hopes someday of being a manager.

Most of the men and women who graduate from the local universities are decidedly middle class. They might have become teachers, but recently education has become overcrowded. These recruits are first-generation university-trained; that is, they probably are the first from their families to attend college. In that respect, they also sanctify the university degree. As to their motivation for joining any bank, much less our bank, I can hear their parents saying, "Why don't you go to work for a bank, or the telephone company, or an insurance company, or Con Ed?" These are symbols of solidity; whoever heard of Bell Telephone going broke, or Chase Manhattan going to the wall? These recruits normally ask only two questions: What salary do they start at and what will they retire at?

Before we actually hire trainees for the assistant manager program, we put them through a security check that borders on invasion of privacy. We check the grades they made in all of their schooling, we go into the type of family they come from, we want to know what kind of home — physically — the trainee was brought up in, we find out how much money his father has in the bank (and which bank). In short, we go above and beyond the call of normal recruitment into prying. I'd say we fall short of Central Intelligence Agency practices, but not by much.

Although we don't use a grading scale per se, the sum effect of the security check is the same as if we graded people as to their background. The report is written in a narrative form, but it contains the entire input of our investigation. It will contain the fact that your father is, let's say, out of work, and on his uppers, or that you come from a poor, middle-income, or upper-income family. The bank claims it doesn't hold the fact against you that you might come from a poor background, but if that's so, why do they bother? What interest is it of the bank? The bank says it wants to have as much information as possible on all of its employees; after all, the bank says, we're dealing with money and you never can be too sure about people who handle money. . . .

Any bank worth its salt would deny the subtle form of discrimination which goes on, more or less, in practically every bank throughout the world. I have a friend who works for a very large British bank, and he says that he is staggered by the automatic and permanent class discrimination that goes on there. If you've graduated from a public school the likes of Harrow, Eton, Winchester, you're automatically a member of the Old Boys' network, and this despite whether you've graduated from university or not. Oxford or Cambridge on top of public school is the frosting on the cake, no matter what you've heard about the London School of Economics.

Our recruiting for the assistant manager's program is discriminatory but nobody is ever aware of it. When our recruiters go beating the bushes at local colleges they never tell the potential recruits that once you're categorized as an assistant manager you're pegged as an assistant manager for life.

We do have another training program available, but we only talk about it to graduates of the Harvard Business School. And the Wharton School of Finance at the University of Pennsylvania, and all of the Ivy League, plus a few schools which don't have the brown-bag stigma. This program is called the credit training program, and this is our West Point — the future leaders of First Mutual Trust come up through the credit program.

Although the style of recruiting for the two programs is

quite different, the investigation we run is the same. And the same kind of thoroughness which goes into the check for those recruits entering the assistant manager's program holds for the credit program trainees. We use the same green form, which carries the recruit's schooling, his parents' net worth (which we get from Dun & Bradstreet or the Commercial Credit Association) and whether the recruit comes from a cold-water tenement (which is unlikely), a middle-class subdivision (also unlikely) or an upper-middle- or upper-class neighborhood. I am embarrassed to say we retain a private detective agency to run checks on all potential officers, be they from the Lower East Side of Manhattan or the Upper East Side. We don't hold anyone's parents against a recruit, but we are very much aware of a recruit whose parents have a net worth into seven figures. We know before we hire whether a college graduate is a social drinker at Yale or a potential drunk from Rutgers.

If your references seem to check out and you don't seem to be a flagrant deadbeat, we ask you to come in for a second interview. (I am counting as the first interview the initial contact made by the recruiter and the applicant.) This second interview is usually an hour long and it is most often conducted by the recruiter who made the initial contact with the applicant. Toward the end the recruiter will usually excuse himself and say that he wants the applicant to "see someone else."

If the two bank officers agree on the applicant, they then send him on to the personnel department and then the bank makes an official offer through personnel. On the other hand, if — to coin a phrase — the cut of the applicant's jib is not quite right for First Mutual Trust's lagoon, the two officers nod at each other and one will say, "Fine, we'll be in touch with you, we've got all the information we need at the moment." *Ciao,* recruit, better luck at First National City.

The tragedy of this recruiting is that the applicant has yet to learn of the scope of the bank. All he knows is that the bank has over a hundred branches, with a main headquarters down in Wall Street. The rosy future which is painted goes like this: after you've finished the training program, you'll be made the assistant manager of a branch, and if things go well you'll eventually end up running your own branch! To those applicants who show an interest in the bank beyond their weekly take-home pay and retirement benefits, the branch manager aspect is emphasized, and the pitch usually goes that the recruit will be running his own multimillion dollar enterprise, responsible for the whole shebang from vault opening to vault closing. But what we don't say, and never will say, is that once a man is placed into branch banking he rarely transfers out of it. You're in there for life, and in some ways it's a bit like signing on for the old French Foreign Legion.

The bank is extremely shrewd when they recruit future officers for this training program. They know they could never get away with this kind of pitch at the Harvard Business School. And in their recruitment they have a tendency to look for people who are diligent, kind, trustworthy (especially trustworthy), but not too bright. The college marks are most acceptable at a B-minus level; anything higher than that and the recruit is going to start asking deeper questions — questions that the bank can't really answer. Is there a life beyond the manager of a branch? Not very likely, because when we get someone through the assistant manager's program and several years into his career, all we want from him is the managership of larger branches. The manager of a branch in the Bronx is not sent to see if the liquid assets of, say, a Lockheed Aircraft Corporation warrant a multimillion dollar loan. (And herein the hypocrisy. After the pieces of the disaster with Lockheed were picked up, all of the banks who lent money to Lockheed when they shouldn't have started looking for scapegoats and unfortunately there weren't any. The banking establishment approved the Lockheed loans, as did the banking establishment approve the lines of credit for that ultimate of Toonerville Trolleys, the Penn Central. I have often wondered if these situations might not have worked out better had a $15,000-a-year branch manager been given the ultimate responsibility. He certainly wouldn't have done worse.)

Our line of patter to the applicants is that they're going to learn all phases of the operations of the bank. An obvious falsehood. What we really mean is that they're going to learn how a teller operates: thus when we have the applicant signed on, we immediately send him through a two-week teller school, which is supposed to train him in all the nuances of tellerdom. After they finish teller school they're shipped to one of our branches where they stand next to an experienced teller for a week and watch. For the second week of on-the-job training they act as the teller with the experienced teller watching them, and for the third, fourth, and fifth weeks they operate as tellers.

Before Women's Lib we started our male trainees at $150 a week and the female trainees at $135. (Our rationale for this bit of sexist thinking being that the men might be sent into the East Bronx or Bedford-Stuyvesant, whereas we wouldn't send the women there.) Now, everyone is paid the same. The fallacy of the program is apparent: these trainees, with their college education, are spending five weeks with people whose future is truly limited — the uneducated teller who is making a lifetime profession of standing behind bars. Although we warn the trainees not to tell the full-time tellers that they are, indeed, trainees and won't be spending the rest of their days on their feet, the trainees are only human: they talk about how soon it will be until they leave this hellish life. The hostility between teller and trainee-teller is immense, and the full-time teller reluctantly teaches the trainee-teller, but I honestly don't know how much the full-timers hold back in the so-called education process.

The real tellers earn no more than $105 to $125 a week, and there are the trainees sporting $150 a week. That, if nothing else, increases the anger that the full-time teller has.

So now we have our trainee standing at his cage just like the other tellers wondering where his or her beautiful training program has gone to. We don't regard these people as trainees at this point; they're bodies, and if they're not fully able-bodied tellers they will do for the moment. The operations executives, those in the bank who are responsible for numbers of branches in given areas and regions, tend to use the trainees as emergency cannon fodder. Has the flu gone through the clerical personnel on Fifty-third Street? Immediately ship over three trainees who can function as tellers. Has there been a stabbing at our Carnegie Hall office? Get the blood off the floor and send in a stout-hearted replacement. (As with all suspiciously apocryphal tales, I hasten to say that this story is touchingly true. One of the tellers in that branch had fallen debits over credits in love with another teller. They were married and eventually the woman quit to raise, I suppose, a little teller. The man stayed on, but it turned out that he had a roving eye. He began a sub rosa romance with another woman who worked at the savings account window. Now all of this would have been fine had not the vault guard been involved. He, it turned out, had once been in love with the woman teller and was deeply hurt when she went and married the male teller. However, like all stoical bank guards, he remained impassive about his loss until the male teller began playing around with the girl at the savings account window. He decided to inform the woman teller who had retired, so he made a discreet telephone call and said to the woman that she had better come into the bank and watch her husband's roving hands and eyes. The woman came in, all right, but she was packing a butcher knife, and the first incision — a neat one — went in her husband. As he watched the blood emerge from the region roughly near the spleen, the woman calmly walked over to the vault guard and got him someplace between the third and fourth ribs. The guard was caught unaware and, indeed, he hadn't even seen the husband go down like an ox. It was at this point that the screaming began; after all, here were two employees of the bank bleeding all over the place, and more important, the vault guard was not functioning. The woman dropped the knife and walked out of the bank, but not before all of the action was spotted by the woman in savings. She tore around the side of her area and chased the ex-teller out onto busy West Fifty-seventh Street, where the two of them started fighting. The stabber was arrested and shipped off to Bellevue to have her head checked; the guard and the male teller were sent to Roosevelt Hospital to have their bodies patched up. And the area operations man, who arrived shortly after all of this to take control, wiped a tear of sentiment out of his eye, got the cleaning crews to work, and ordered two trainees to come into the branch to work as tellers.)

The point here is simply that we treat the trainees who have spent five or six weeks as tellers as minor league third basemen: we transfer them throughout the metropolitan New York area to fill any personnel gaps we might have.

Because the clerical and operations personnel of the bank don't give a damn about the bank, they are forever falling prey to sicknesses, minor or otherwise, and we are forever falling short of personnel. The trainees who have a smattering of experience as tellers are thrown into the breach. This tends to unsettle the trainees — they graduated from college and now they're being shuttled around — and they're forever ringing up the personnel department asking what the hell is going on. Personnel hems and haws and tells the trainees that the next step up our ladder is the general cage clerk school, but that unfortunately this school does not run on a regular basis.

The general cage in a bank is where the more sophisticated but boring money transactions take place: letters of credit, transfers of money, cashier's checks, and so forth. For a regular teller who tries to get ahead in our little world, it usually takes a good five years before he's moved from a teller's window through school over to the general cage. But the trainee breezes into the general cage school after no more than a few months. Needless to say, there is resentment in the general cage when the trainee finishes the general cage clerk school and starts to work.

The general cage school lasts three weeks, but it has no fixed schedule: it operates to its own private and mysterious inner music. Although it should be axiomatic that as soon as a trainee finishes one phase of training, he be moved into another, the reality is quite the opposite. Trainees can wait around for months for a general cage clerk school to convene.

After cage clerk school comes the platform assistants seminar. The platform is that raised or separated portion of any bank where the officers are seated. It usually is carpeted, and there are secretaries for the more senior officers depending on the size of the branch. In olden times (in banking, like much of the rest of the financial world, the delineation is the Great Depression) the platform in many banks was exactly that: a deliberately raised portion of the banking floor which set the officers apart from hoi polloi.

You can usually spot the head officer of a large branch on the platform: his desk is out in the open, but barely. And to reach him you have to run a gauntlet of junior officers and platform assistants. There is a variety of business conducted on the platform, ranging from six-figure loans to big and valued customers to drifters who float through trying to lay a bad check on you. New accounts are opened, overdrawn accounts are shut, and the life of the branch flows through the platform. In some banks, the officers and platform personnel are physically removed from the banking floor, but the tradition is the same: a very rigid desk and pecking order, with the top officer sitting far away from the rabble.

The platform assistants seminar is held at the main office of the bank in Wall Street. One of the problems here is that a part of the platform assistants seminar is a four-day briefing with the installment loan division. This is fine, except the installment loan division people are not particularly happy about giving up four days of their time in the middle of the summer, so invariably they're canceling out their portion of the platform assistants seminar during the months of July and August. A trainee might have finished teller school, general cage school, and be ready for the platform seminar and still have to sit around waiting for the summer to end and the seminar to begin.

At the absolute worst, a trainee can start with the bank on January 1 and finish teller school in two weeks. But it may be a couple of months before there are enough people to convene a general cage clerk school, so let's say the trainee doesn't start until sometime in April. It is mid-May when that school is over and personnel may decide to ship the trainee out to a branch for a little practical experience until June. At the first sight of spring, however, the platform seminar heads for the beach and our trainee could be kept cooling his heels until September. Ideally, we should put people through this training in no more than three months, surely less than six months. When we start approaching nine months (which is closer to the norm) we aren't doing anyone any good.

Depending on the country's economic conditions, we enroll anywhere from 75 to 125 trainees in the assistant manager's program in a given year. But at least 60 of them will drop out, and I don't know whether it's because of inability or because they suddenly see they've become chattels to the bank. We certainly don't deliberately design the program to lose people, but because we don't watch over it with any care, we lose people we have made an investment in.

For those who traipse around the bank and manage to finish the entire training program without losing their mind or their patience, the problems are just beginning. We put the graduates to work on the platforms and they're elbow to elbow with people who have worked like dogs to make the platform. Most people on the platform who have not come into the bank as trainees have worked for us for at least fifteen years. That's five tough years as a teller, perhaps another three or four years as a head teller, and still another stretch working in the general cage. To these people who have devoted their life to the bank, the platform is a sacred goal, not an achievement to be taken lightly. To say that there is friction between the trainees and the long-time employees is an understatement. The old employees bitterly resent the trainees; the trainees, who've been bogged down in a time-consuming, ill-conceived training program, regard the old-timers as hopeless and out of fashion.

The personnel department, keeping tabs on the trainees, is sent monthly progress reports. The older employees invariably submit poor ratings and reports. The trainees, having spent close to a year with us, are wondering where their dream went: Where is the bank branch they're going to manage? They are gradually beginning to understand that they've been had, that they're not going to be running a branch all by themselves in no time. They see that the large branches are multimillion dollar operations trusted to full vice presidents of the bank, officers who have lending power up to and sometimes above $250,000. Even the smaller branches are staffed by experienced line officers.

It is at this point that the trainees start bombarding the personnel department with requests for transfers. The three most popular areas are international banking, because everyone would like to work in London or Paris; public relations, because even the trainees can see that not much is going on in that department; and finally, personnel itself.

The logic, I suppose, is that if a trainee got screwed so badly, why doesn't he get into the department that does the screwing? The situation gets compounded because the operations men in the bank regard the trainees who have finished the program just the way they regard the trainees who have completed teller school: a body is a body when you need it. We do possess a group of people euphemistically called the platform pool, which simply means a large and floating body of people trained for platform work. And float is what they do: Staten Island for a month, the wonders of the East Bronx for three months, darkest Brooklyn for six months. The ex-trainee, wondering what the hell he is doing as he contemplates the variations of the New York City subway system, keeps asking where his very own branch is. Personnel replies that it's coming, it's coming, but we don't have a permanent position yet. One ex-trainee once told me that Dante's vision had nothing on being a floating platform person in Queens.

We've been running this alleged training program for seven years and to date it has been an unqualified disaster. Resentment has gradually been building between graduates of the program and employees who have worked themselves up by their bootstraps. It does not pay to have two warring factions in any bank, large or small, and yet this is what we are approaching. We've also found that after a few years the graduates of the program simply leave us; they see that even though they've been promoted to the first step — assistant treasurer — they also know for sure that their life for the next thirty years or so is completely set in a preordained pattern. And they don't buy it.

The young people today graduating from any college, no matter how humble or local or newly arrived, have an entirely different outlook on life than any earlier generation. They are not the type to join a bank and wait for the gold watch at retirement. If they're bored, or if they feel they've been taken, they'll simply leave. Mobility is the key word today and most banks haven't realized it. Although the officer turnover at First Mutual Trust does not equal the 50 percent turnover of the clerical staff, it has been rising steadily in recent years and will continue to rise. The bank, unfortunately, does not see or acknowledge the trend and in a few years a truly desperate middle management personnel shortage is going to occur.

Our second major training program, the credit school, is, as I have said, our West Point. We screen applicants to the credit school with a great deal of care, and everyone who applies must take a battery of entrance exams — basic accounting tests. You can't get into the credit school unless you can add and subtract. If you can multiply and divide and play around with graphs, so much the better. Most of the applicants to the credit school come from prestige business schools. We will almost do handsprings to attract a graduate from Yale, and all we ask of him is that he can walk, talk, and button his pants correctly. We're historically in love with Yale, for reasons that are obscured in boola-boola history, and we'll let them into the credit school if they show *any* aptitude whatsoever.

I am quite fond of the large Yale contingent at our bank except for their squash racquets. The Yalies are forever waltzing around the halls with their racquets at lunchtime, hopping over to the Brook Club or the Racquet & Tennis Club for a quick game. The one thing about a squash player is that he wants you to know that he's a squash player, and they are continually banging your knees and elbows with their goddam racquets in the elevator. (It has been said that one of our motives in signing up as many Yale graduates as we do is that they invariably *look* like what the public thinks a banker should look like.)

The credit school lasts four months and there is no monkeying around about when it starts or when it finishes. It is as demanding as any college-level course and it familiarizes the credit trainee with all of the aspects of credit that a banker must know. When a trainee is finished with the school, he knows how to take any company's balance sheet and analyze it and especially pick up anything that is shaky. He also will know whether a company is worth extending credit to, and how much credit, and how to distinguish real assets from tanks full of imaginary oil.

It is a difficult course, and when we take the sixty or so each year for it, we intend that they will become credit officers and eventually the leaders of the bank. The tests given to the trainees at the end of the course are difficult and we don't allow gentlemen's Cs, we want high marks.

The salaries of the trainees who start out in the assistant manager's program and the credit school will give you an inkling of the difference in attitudes. The assistant manager's trainees begin at $150 a week; the credit school trainees begin at $12,000 a year and go up rapidly. We never take a trainee headed for the assistant manager's program to lunch. We always take the credit school trainees to lunch in our executive dining room. And although the food in the executive dining room is catered by Stouffer's, it still is the executive dining room, which is an area that few people out of the assistant manager's program will ever see.

If, God forbid, someone fails the credit school course —

and about 15 percent a year do fail — we have a slight problem. We truly would like him to leave quietly and bother someone else. So if the trainee stupidly insists on staying with the bank, then we cheerfully transfer him to the assistant manager's program. Six months' exposure to the horrors of that usually drives him out of the bank. Aside from the 15 percent who flunk out, another 15 percent are disillusioned with this initial view of banking, and they simply quit and go elsewhere.

The remainder are crackerjack people and have a bright future with us, or, truly, in any other bank. As soon as they leave the credit school, they're handed an assignment, usually assisting a lending officer at a large branch. There is no idle shifting around of these people; we treat them gingerly and with a great deal of respect.

At first, they do all the backup work regarding large loans — the double-checking of credit and balance sheets. After about four or five months of this kind of work, they're put out on the platform, handling credit work by themselves. Within a year they'll be promoted to assistant treasurer. In four or five years they will have become vice presidents, and they will either have been slated to become top credit officers of the bank or eventually they will be handed the plums in the metropolitan banking division: the Fifth Avenue and Park Avenue branches, the major Wall Street branches. The graduates of the credit school are not necessarily well connected but their heads are well connected. I have a great deal of respect for credit officers: it's not an easy job at all and by and large they perform it well. They are laying it on the line every day in terms of granting or not granting million dollar loans. The companies seeking the loans — and their auditors, who are in themselves a special breed — are not always totally suffused with honesty. The banks on the receiving end of the loan requests from companies must be careful and tactful, an uneasy combination of traits.

No one is infallible, and the credit officer who begins to stretch his luck is eventually removed from the most sensitive jobs. If, for example, an officer with what is essentially a credit background makes several large loans which suddenly begin to smell, he will be removed from a large branch to a less active branch. You can't do much damage lending money out in Maspeth, Queens, or at least not as much as you can on Fifth Avenue. However, when this kind of overt demotion occurs, the officer usually gets the drift immediately and starts looking for another job. We might suggest that he switch from the loan division over to the branch division, but this kind of notion is usually met with disdain.

Besides the assistant manager's training program and the credit school, First Mutual Trust has a very quiet, little-known third form of recruiting which is laughingly called "placement." Placement, that is, of people who know people. I call this our Binky-Stinky training program, because it seems that many of those recruited are known by hoary prep school names, which have a certain dated charm. We do indeed have a Binky working for us, and indeed, a Stinky as well. Also a Buzzy.

I mentioned earlier, a bit jocularly, that a $2,000,000 portfolio with us never hurt anyone's chances at getting a job at a bank, and this is absolutely true — and not only with ourselves, but with many other major banks as well. If we have our hands on $2,000,000, that will more than pay the going rate for a vice president. Of course, if the nephew is a closet case, it can be a little disappointing. But if the guy can function at all, if he shows the slightest glimmer of talent, why there's jubilation. Now you certainly cannot walk into the bank dragging your sniveling nephew behind you, and nowhere will anyone admit that so much on deposit with a bank is worth so much in terms of a job. But my unofficial guess is that a million dollar portfolio is the break-even figure: under that it can become a headache, over that and it really works.

Placement has its own jargon, its own style of interviewing, its own accents. The officer who is interviewing the nephew would never be so gauche as to ask who the rich uncle is; but the nephew isn't stupid, he knows the fix is on and at the opportune time he'll casually mention that his uncle has an account at the bank. The nephew knows. I once sat in on one of these interviews and it was from another world.

"Ah, what did you specialize in at Harvard?" asked the interviewer.

"Ancient history, actually," said the nephew.

"Ah, did you ever take any finance courses by any chance?"

"No." No explanation, no justification, just a straight-ahead no.

"Ah, do you suppose you would be interested in bank accounting?" The tone of voice implied that financing was a terrific and nifty thing to spent your time on. But the kid was too smart.

"Well . . . I suppose I could *try* financing to see if I could get interested in it . . ." Said with little if any enthusiasm. That nephew is going to go a long way.

Things are more cut and dried when the money is ac-

tually in the hands of the beholder; that's real money as far
as the bank is concerned, not money controlled by a distant
uncle. Our classic case is an officer named Burton. He is
very dumb but comes from a very good family. He lives with
his wife and children in a lovely house in Scarsdale,
and as far as he's concerned the world ends at the northern
boundary of Scarsdale. Every day he gets on the bankers'
special, which breezes into Grand Central Station about
10:00 A.M. or so. He wears flannel suits, with vests, summer
and winter, and lest you think he's a snob, let me report
that he brings his lunch to work every day in a brown
paper bag, eats his lunch in the executive dining room,
folds his paper bag and takes it home every night to Scarsdale. I think he gets about two weeks to a single paper bag.
Nobody kids Burton about the paper bag; in fact, nobody
kids Burton at all. Burton's personal portfolio is with our
bank and the last time I looked into its worth it was about
$5,000,000. We don't make fun of $5,000,000 portfolios,
and as far as we're concerned the more paper bags like that
the better we like it.

It is quite a problem keeping Burton busy so he thinks
he's needed, and yet it is crucial to keep him away from
any kind of job that he will make a mess of. So far we've
tried him in personnel, and that didn't work, publicity and
that didn't work, and now we're putting Burton in charge
of mailing lists. He's our mailing list officer and we all fer-
vently hope that he likes mailing lists.

Of course there are risks building a career around wealth
alone, whether it's your own, your wife's, or your uncle's.
One of the most influential officers in the bank was a man
named Rodney. He was a millionaire but he also had talent, and he headed one of our largest divisions. Unfortu-

nately he did not like his mother. Now I for one am all for not liking your mother, if you're a little cool on mothers generally. His mother, however, was worth $4,000,000 and that's at least one good reason for sending Mom a Mother's Day card. But this man didn't; he claimed to one and all that his mother was a crazy. Mom kept her mouth shut, which is what her son should have done, and Mom finally died and cut Rodney out of her will. It must have been quite a scene because the struggle over the $4,000,000 made page three of the *New York Daily News*. Mom left all $4,000,000 to a dog and cat cemetery and the only thing that the son could get his hands on was a tatty villa somewhere in Italy. She loved dogs and cats but she really hated her son.

Thank God for Rodney that his father had left him a pretty good piece of change, all of which is in the bank's competent hands. Nonetheless, the very top officers are keeping a closer eye than usual on Rodney.

# CHAPTER V

I GREW up in Hobokcn, and before my family moved to the tranquillity of Nutley, New Jersey, I became acquainted with some of the more colorful characters around the Hoboken docks — the docks that were celebrated far and wide in the movie *On the Waterfront*. One of the more distinctive characteristics of the Hoboken docks is loansharking, or, "I'll give you five [five dollars] for six [six dollars] until payday." This meant that the loan shark, or lending officer, lent you five dollars with the implicit understanding that you would return six dollars to him when you were paid on Friday. And no collateral was involved, either. You didn't sign anything, there were no embarrassing questions; just take the money and have a good time. Of course if you didn't return the money on Friday you had an arm broken. In those instances where the loans were larger (thus making the risk to the lender commensurately larger), if you didn't pay the loan back you were liable to have two arms broken, and a bruised kidney thrown in for good measure.

If you hung around the docks of Hoboken for any length of time you quickly understood the lending policy on the waterfront and you knew which characters were the lenders, which were the enforcers, and which were the accountants. Imagine my surprise, then, when one day a couple of years ago I walked into the installment lending section of the bank to deliver some papers and was suddenly in Déja Vu City. There, in the flesh, was a character from my childhood, one Tony Corallostein, son of a notorious loan shark named Angelo Corallostein who was a legendary figure when I was a child. (A word about the ethnic makeup of Corallostein: someplace in his distant heritage someone named Stein merged with someone named Corallo. On the docks they felt that Corallostein had the best of both worlds for his chosen profession: the astute economic abilities of Stein and the physical agility of Corallo. Pop fit the bill. Unfortunately, young Tony Corallostein not only was unable to comprehend compound interest, he also had a glass jaw which shattered with alarming regularity.)

One other thing should be noted about Tony Corallostein: he was a gorilla. Scarred face, hulky body, Tony had arms which swung perilously close to the ground, and although the day I saw him he was wearing the semblance of a blue suit and a white shirt, he really couldn't conceal the fact that he was a gorilla. "Hey baby, how ya doin', long time no see," he said to me. I looked around nervously, wondering what in God's name Tony was up to in the sacred reaches of First Mutual Trust Company. I asked Tony what he was doing in *my* bank. "Why, I'm a collection officer," he said with a tinge of asperity in his voice. "I'm in today to go over some numbers."

That intelligence staggered me and I pressed Tony to the employees cafeteria to find out what gave. In the fifteen years or so since I had seen Tony, he had led a checkered career doing nothing. His glass jaw and his gross stupidity rendered him unfit for work with his father on the docks. He had decided to go straight and somehow he had managed to get a job with a loan company, not unlike Household Finance, or Beneficial Finance, or Seaboard Finance. As any radio listener will testify, these finance companies advertise extensively and lend money with less collateral than most banks: they also charge rates which are much higher. Although most bankers turn up their noses at loan companies, while turning up their noses they do an extremely brisk business lending their money to loan companies, which in turn lend the money out again. It turned out that Tony had had a sparkling career with, I'll call it Happy Finance Company ("Don't Be Sappy, Borrow from Happy"). And sure enough, he had moved from Happy Finance to First Mutual Trust in our collection division of installment loans.

The regular officers at First Mutual Trust look upon the installment loan division as something to be avoided at all costs. It is grubby, the people are scruffy, and it is not in keeping with our own self-image as bankers. But somewhere in the recesses of the executive suite, a genius has decided that one of the best sources of manpower to staff the loan department is finance companies, thus gorillas like Tony loll around the premises. Needless to say, we would absolutely never put the strong arm on a customer who had defaulted on a loan. But can you imagine the look on someone's face when the likes of Tony gently inquired about past payments?

Ex-finance company people make very good loan officers. First of all, they're so relieved to be away from the horrors of a Household Finance, or a Beneficial, that when they hit First Mutual Trust Company they think they're in seventh heaven. In a finance company, the way of life is perpetual dunning: nobody ever meets their payments and all the people do is dun. Although we dun, we do it by telephone, and the collection guys are not expected to go up five-flight walkups to collect on bad loans. We have had a few problems in the past when some of them have become, in our delicate, restrained, throat-clearing parlance, "enthusiastic." But we get rid of such offenders immediately. "Uh, Aspromonte was a bit, how shall I say it, enthusiastic," said a first vice president, referring to a collection officer who threatened to throw a laggard widow in front of the Lexington Avenue express. That's enthusiastic.

Tony, it seems, had become one of our ace collectors of defaulted loans, and I am positive much of his success was due to his voice. Just discussing a loan over the phone he must have put the fear of God into the customer, and no way would they ever think of defaulting.

Most of us at one time or another have gone into a bank for a loan. Large banks in metropolitan areas everywhere depend on the enormous revenues generated by personal loans. And most of us, when we go into our bank for a loan, are embarrassed by the fact that we do need a loan. Not surprisingly, conversations in our personal loan department are conducted in hushed tones, and since the customer is asking us for something, he usually is nervous.

We have: auto loans, car repair loans, boat loans, household improvement loans, get-ready-because-here-comes-the-baby loans, renovate-the-second-home loans, fix-the-plumbing loans, and perhaps a dozen other tags for what are all essentially personal loans. Our in-house memorandum to employees about our loan program says: "First Mutual Trust Company has always been a leader in developing new methods to resolve the problems of commercial banking and the implementation of the numerical credit scoring system represents another step in this direction. This system has been designed with the knowledge that good credit analysis cannot be prepackaged for every loan. Therefore, it is intended only for a screen device prior to regular credit analysis." On top of that memorandum is stamped this warning, "Confidential for bank use only. Do not discuss with or show to the customer." We may be a leader in working out a loan system, but don't tell the customer about it.

The crucial thing to keep in mind about our loan policy is that no matter what we say, no matter how much we do protest, and despite all of our palaver about lending money to shufflin', grinnin' darkies, we really only want to lend money to middle-class whites, and in the final analysis we are truly happiest lending money for either automobiles or boats. Essentially, we want to lend money to overachieving, advertising-oriented white males who will take our money and buy a material object which will depreciate and then fall apart at the end of the thirty-six-month loan. Just in time to start the cycle over again.

If you've ever gone into a bank seeking a loan, you will be glad to know the process is practically the same everywhere. At First Mutual we ask the customer to fill out a loan application; it's a seemingly innocent document. After the application is completed, a receptionist asks the customer to wait a minute — "our loan representatives are busy at the moment, but someone will be with you shortly." What is happening at this moment is not that the loan reps are killing themselves with work: they're taking the loan application and applying to it an extremely simple but unintentionally biased set of standards.

We first want to know whether you've ever taken out a loan with First Mutual Trust. And we can find out immediately if you had what we call an "unsatisfactory loan," which means you tried to stiff us, or a "satisfactory loan," which means you showed up at our bank every month on the dot with the little loan payment booklet. If your loan was satisfactory, you get 40 points; unsatisfactory, a minus 40. If you've never had a loan with us before, there are neither points given nor taken away.

Then we want to know where you live — although on the application form it's an innocuous address listing. If you've only lived at your present address for a year or less, you don't get any points. But if you've been living there from one to four years, we give you 15 points, and anything beyond five years is worth 25 points. Although we don't penalize you for not living at your current address for more than a year, we reward generously the fact that you might well be a sloth and haven't had the energy to get out and find a new home. It is a negative reward, in a way, and in our minds it helps to screen out the shiftless who, obviously, are not deserving of loans.

From home to telephone. If you don't have a telephone at your residence, you lose 25 points. And if you do have a telephone, we don't add or subtract points from your total. We have nothing on our loan application which covers a telephone which is installed but which is out of order most of the time due to the atherosclerosis of Bell Telephone.

As far as your job goes, we want you regularly employed. We're not interested in anyone who's itinerant — either at home or at work. If you've just gone to work, no points; if you've been there from one to four years, 15 points, and if you managed to hang on to your job for five years or more, 25 points. But 25 is the top as far as we're concerned; we are not impressed with gold watches. When it comes to salary, we look at gross monthly salary. We don't give any points from 0 to $249 a month; from $250 to $499 you get 10 points; $500 to $749 20 points, and anything above $750, 30 points. But no more beyond that. We'll give a customer 20 points for a special checking account, 20 points for a savings account, 30 points for a regular checking account. The hypocrisy here is that if you have any astuteness when it comes to money management, you will have your savings in a savings and loan association, because they invariably pay higher interest rates. And regular checking accounts, with their minimum balance of $500 required, are another banking ripoff. What we're really saying is, bank stupidly with us and we will gladly reward your stupidity.

At the bottom of the application is a box which should be checked if the loan is for the purchase of a car. We'll give you 25 points if you want to buy a car, but no points if for any other purpose. I own a car, and while I don't regard it as a sex symbol, it does have its uses; I could survive without it, too. But the mere fact that we assign a weighted value to it of 25 points is sheer madness. Simply, we regard wanting to buy a car as equivalent to working on your job for five years or more and as almost equal to the highest salary covered by our point system. Fostering the American automotive industry I suppose is next to clean armpits, mother, and God, but as far as I'm concerned it shows a massive misunderstanding about what banks should be doing in the private sector.

Now if everyone has grasped the point system, take my word that it is almost like grading an exam. You quickly run down the customer's application adding or subtracting under the point system until you get a total. (We assume that our loan representatives can add and subtract properly.) After the loan officer has reached the bottom of the form he has his total, and all he has to do is apply it against the guidelines. We classify the total as either low, medium, or high. A score of 40 points or less indicates that the applicant is liable to be a bad risk and if we can ever be talked into granting him a loan we need to have a promissory note signed by a co-signer, guaranteeing the note. If the customer scores above 80 points, he's in: he'll get his loan without any problems. In fact, if we turn down a loan and the applicant has 80 points or more, the branch has to justify its decision to the installment loan division. Whenever the score hits between 41 and 79, an explanatory note must be written telling headquarters whether the loan was accepted or rejected and why.

We don't lend money if the applicant is involved in any kind of litigation; we don't lend money if he has high fixed expenses even though he might have a high income. We don't lend money under any circumstance to anyone whom we think has ever manhandled a bank before. Our little scoring sheet makes no distinction whatsoever if a man owns his own home. God forbid a single girl comes in who shares an apartment with a friend. If their telephone just happens to be in the girl friend's name, the girl will have a difficult time getting her loan. Unlisted telephones don't stir us to action; we've got to see it listed in the telephone book to believe it. We dislike applicants who don't have a personal home telephone but happen to have a business phone. Ditto for answering services in some company's name.

We — and just about every other bank in the country — don't like to lend money to barbers, bartenders, beauticians, musicians, actors, writers, cooks, waiters, waitresses, countermen, employees of foreign governments, hospital attendants, hotel employees, longshoremen, dockworkers, porters, salesmen on a straight commission, nurses not connected with hospitals, and people in any other occupation which falls into what we lovingly call the "problem category." It might have occurred to you that some of the categories are in the lower economic scale of this country and you would be correct. And you might further perceive that quite a few of the porters, hospital attendants, waiters, and so forth, are of a skin which is slightly darker in hue than that of First Mutual Trust Company. Right again. But we're not prejudiced, we love our fellow men, we just won't lend these categories the bread.

Chase Manhattan had been running a particularly syrupy set of television commercials about a black photographer who wanted to go into business and open a studio but who didn't have a pfennig to his name. But, says the announcer, Chase stepped in and what you see on the screen is Chase's black photographer jumping all over his studio engaging in "high fashion work." It's more high camp than high fashion, and although obviously Chase did indeed set the fellow up, we wouldn't. We'd say photography is a "problem category" and would say no. Politely, with all of our teeth showing, but no.

One day I asked an officer at the bank why we seemed to

have so many "problem category" loans. The officer pointed out that I was quite wrong; we didn't have any loans in the problem category, we simply didn't make the loan. Of course if Andrew Wyeth, an artist, stepped in and asked for a loan of $5,000, he would probably get it, but first you'd have to explain to someone like a Tony Corallostein who Wyeth is, that his paintings are grabbed off the walls of the Knoedler Gallery whenever he has a showing, and that his collateral is so good that he probably could bail us out of a tight weekend whenever we were doing a little strange floating of cash on hand. Vidal Sassoon, the British hairdresser who seems to be all over the lot? Sorry, Vidal, can't spare a shilling on your occupation, but when we learn that you've got salons on prime Madison Avenue property, that's a different spit curl.

The bank — all banks — feel that artists are unstable, cooks, waiters, and busboys are unstable, musicians unstable, ambassadors from Hungary are unstable, writers are unstable, bartenders and bargirls and barflies are unstable. Congressional Medal of Honor winners get a pat on the back from us, but unless they're commissioned officers they're unstable. When we go into the hospital, we sure want the hospital attendant to take the goddam bedpan, but sorry, no dinero. We're not paranoid, but in our little world of loans much of the world is unstable.

In addition to the problem categories, we're against short anything. Short residence at your current address, short-term employee. We're not happy with single people; give us a married man in hock to his ears. We don't like people who change their jobs too often; we're unhappy if the only previous loan experience you've had is with one of those phony "bill-consolidation" loans from the finance company.

If we're pressed by a persistent busboy for a loan, we'll tell him if he can get a co-maker to sign the loan as well, we'll think about it. But the co-maker has to be upright and proper. And our guidelines say that quite explicitly. They note, however, that "too much reliance should not be placed on a co-maker." In other words, even if the busboy does get someone who is reliable in our eyes, we're still not very happy. Essentially, we don't think it is sound banking practice to rely entirely on a co-maker. And if our busboy walks into the bank with the white, wealthy owner of the restaurant he works in, that's not good either. In our view, the restaurant could fall on hard times and then the owner is not much of a co-maker.

Let us say, hypothetically, that you get enough points on our scale, that you've been living at your current address long enough, that you've been working at your job long enough, that you're not a member of the Romanian consulate, that the purpose of the loan is to buy a new car — let's assume all of these factors. Do we simply sit there and hand you $4,000 in new green? Of course not. The loan representative tells you that everything looks okay, but since it is your initial application it has to be sent to the installment loan division for approval. The officer sends you out of the bank with the cheery message that you'll be hearing from the bank in a day or two and that everything is fine. What he doesn't tell you is that we are now about to check your credit.

All banks use some form of a credit check on an individual applying for a loan. We, like many New York banks, use a company called the Credit Data Corporation, and they have on a computer all information pertaining to bankruptcies, judgments against you, suits pending against you, liens against you. Everything that might be in the public record. We simply say that all installment applications must be cleared with Credit Data Corporation.

Actually, every loan folder contains a sheet for the Credit Data clearance, and before the branch sends the loan folder up to the installment loan division it has to have the clearance. Even though Credit Data might approve the credit rating of the applicant, the bank still can turn the loan down.

Where any credit rating service can really be insidious is in its impersonal, computerized, nonhuman approach to everything — and in its memory. A friend of mine applied for a charge account at a New York department store not long ago and was told flatly that he couldn't have the charge, he was a bad risk. This upset my friend considerably and he asked me to find out if I could what the problem was. I called the department store, told them I was from the bank, and found out that they used the Eezee Kwik Kredit Chek Company of Long Island. I then called Eezee Kredit, again telling them that I worked for First Mutual Trust, and asked them to tell me about my friend's situation. I was told that twelve years ago — in 1961 — my friend had earned his bad credit rating from Gregarious Finance Company.

I talked to my friend and asked him if he ever had had any trouble with Gregarious Finance. He thought for a moment and said that the only dealings he ever had had with them was when his father had died in 1961. He said his father had become very ill in 1960 and was in a terrible financial bind. A bank wouldn't lend him the money so he had gone to Gregarious. Gregarious, in view of the father's health, demanded a co-signer and the son reluctantly signed. Needless to say, whenever a finance company lends you money, you also take out insurance which covers every possibility, including lava flows, tidal waves, killer typhoons, and any other act of nature designed to keep the company from collecting their money.

Well, the illness drained the father of all his money, including the loan, and the loan company began badgering the son for the money. The son pointedly told Gregarious to get lost; his point of view during the family crisis was that his father was going to die soon, and the insurance would cover the loan when the poor man finally passed on. The loan company hated this but there wasn't much that they could do. The man died within a few months; by this time the loan was three months in arrears. The loan insurance took effect and paid off the balance of the loan and the son went sadly on his way, never thinking about it. Until a short time ago.

Back in 1961 Gregarious put the son's name on the bad debt list for faulting on the loan during those interim three months, even though they collected every cent they were owed. Despite the fact that my friend had a good job, the black mark stayed quietly on his record in the computer of Eezee Kwik Kredit Chek until he wanted to get a charge account. It took a threatening letter from my friend to the friendly folks at Eezee Kwik to remove the record of the twelve-year-old squabble. And then, dragging their heels every inch of the way, Eezee Kwik sent a letter to the department store where my friend wanted to open the account, apologizing for the entire affair. What Eezee Kwik didn't say was whether they ever removed the defaulted loan from their computer file. Nowadays, the bank must inform you of the reasons for the black mark and you are entitled to see their credit report.

The average middle-class citizen of this country is probably plugged into more than a dozen different charge cards, department store accounts, and credit plans of one form or another. Plus an immense number of subscriptions to book clubs, record clubs, magazines. I don't know of anyone walking on God's green earth who hasn't had a fight with somebody at some time over his account. Depending on the outcome of your particular battle, your credit future may well be at stake. Let us say, for example, that you become embroiled with the American Express computer. This is well within the realm of reality. Let us say also, hypothetically, that American Express and you reach an impasse over a bill and you finally say, "Buzz off, American Express, I'm not paying. Sue me." Unless the bill is of stupendous proportions, American Express will write you off as a bad debt. But (and it's a very large but) although they might write you off, they also might call you a bad credit risk. If they do, suddenly your name will appear on the deadbeat file of a credit company's computer and you will have one hell of a time in the future obtaining credit on anything.

The computer file doesn't know that you and American Express went to the mat in what you thought was a moral victory; the computer couldn't care less. All it knows is that you're a wrongo. Ten years later you might well be applying for a trial membership in the Water Pik of the Month Club and be mysteriously turned down. Not fair, you say? You bet you it's not fair, but it's the system which has enveloped the United States and much of the world today and there is no way of changing it.

If it's hard to escape the ubiquitousness of the computer, it's practically impossible to sort the trouble out with a credit company. In the case of Eezee Kwik Kredit Chek, it wasn't that difficult, because they were out on Long Island and they weren't that large a credit organization. In dealing with a much larger company, the problems of computer retrieval are proportionally more difficult.

But to continue with our loan procedure . . .

Not only do you have to fill out the application, go through an interview, and get a credit check for a loan from us, but we also don't trust anyone's identification. Which is probably correct. *The importance of proper identification cannot be overemphasized,* says one of our guides to loan officers. *Identification of all applicants must be obtained by the interviewer and that can best be accomplished by submission of canceled check with the applicant's signature or an automobile driver's license with a signature.*

Our grim outlook on personal, unsecured loans carries over to other loans you can get from your bank. If your collateral stinks and you've got to get a secured loan with a co-maker, the co-maker has to sign right below your signature and the print is so small on that loan that your co-maker better be wearing strong glasses. Are your teeth rotting, are your gums nice and musty? Come to us for a dental loan. In the case of what we at the bank call cavity money, the dentist has to give you an estimate of the work to be done, and our check on the loan is made out to both of you. I don't know what happens if you happen to default on a dental loan: maybe they come after the gold in your teeth.

The loan to stay away from is the collateral loan, where you put up either your savings account passbook, stocks, bonds, or insurance with cash value against your defaulting on the loan. The reason to avoid this kind of loan at all costs is that the bank is holding property of yours with value, and God forbid if you get sick during the course of the loan. Your stocks will be sold out, your insurance will be cashed in, your savings account will be stripped — to meet the loan payments. I have a friend who put up his savings passbook with $3,000 for a two-year $3,000 loan. Although you don't physically place your passbook in someone like Corallostein's hands, it is placed in a collateral file in the vault where someone like Tony can get at it. In the middle of a divorce settlement which cost my friend more than he thought it would, he had a nervous breakdown and had to be carted away. Nervous breakdowns fall on deaf ears at First Mutual Trust, and at other banks as well. Just like Broadway, the show — or in this case, the payments — must go on. When my friend got out of the hospital and on his feet eighteen months later, he found that his savings account had $750 left in it. Installment loan divisions of any bank have a tendency to panic. No matter that the stock of yours they're holding is at a five-year low, they sell.

When you look at our loan policy in its entirety, from application to credit screening to types of collateral, the only conclusion you can come to is we're not for the poor. Give us not your homeless or your bedraggled, give us your accountant with 2.4 children living slightly over his head on Long Island. Banks have no real faith in the poor. Banks have never had faith in the poor. Banks do, however, have a vision of America — a WASP vision of what America should be: everybody married, working, with slightly more than two children; everyone with a telephone and a bank account. The bank's blank spots are single persons, male and female; retired people, because they might up and die on us; and people who fall into that enormous net called creativity. And, naturally, those poor people who can't get a loan from us go to the finance companies: they get their loan with no difficulty and it's our money (ours in the generic sense) because, as I mentioned earlier, we're busily lending the finance companies money to re-lend. There is a gross hypocrisy here — not a conspiracy, because that word is too encompassing and too strong — but a hypocrisy which contradicts all of the pleasant and heartwarming commercials you see on television for full-service banks.

If First Mutual Trust has the likes of a Tony Corallostein working as a loan rep, then you know some strange things take place in that division. Believe it or not, one of the prerequisites for getting a loan at our bank is being nice and looking nice. This, I grant you, sounds crazy, but if you're not nice to the loan representative he's not going to be nice to you. If the loan representative has a hangover it's not nice to talk so loudly that his head will ring. Remember, you are asking a guy making $150 a week before take-home pay to lend you some money — he's your line of communication with that big faceless institution called the bank.

In addition to hungover loan reps, we have occasionally had loan representatives with active glands. One representative in particular would take advantage of lovely young things who knew nothing about how the processing of a loan worked. A girl would come in and fill out the papers for a $1,000 loan, let's say, and the man would look at her more carefully than at her application and tell her to come back in a day or so and he'd have word for her. Now that's nonsense, because we always phone or send a letter to let the applicant know whether his loan has been okayed or not. Anyhow, the girls would come trotting in and the officer would be Mr. Gloom, telling the girl who

wanted to get away from it all in Puerto Rico for a couple
of weeks that her loan application had been turned down.
The girls would usually be quite upset, and the man would
always try to offer consolation. In addition to consolation,
he'd say, "What I could do is talk to a couple of my friends.
. . . Why don't we have drinks tonight and I'll let you know
what progress I made." In New York City, where bribery is
a way of life and the casting couch can rear its head in the
damnedest places, this kind of a pitch is usually understood. Since most of the secretaries in New York know a
fourflusher when they see one, and since they all recognize
a proposition when it's tossed their way, our fellow had a
very busy social life.

It pains me to say that he got away with this small-time
ploy for quite a while. His scheme fell apart when he became another of the growing number of people in the city
who are overachievers. Not only was he sleeping with girls
who wanted loans, but he had the unmitigated gall to start
taking kickbacks from men who had been applying for
loans. It was this duality which was his undoing. A couple
of girls complained about his loan technique; in my mind,
though, he was probably as bad in bed as he was at making
loans, which is why the complaints started to come in. The
bank, in the normal course of our gumshoe operation,
would have investigated the women's complaints and we
might or might not have done anything about them. Like
rape, the charge is difficult to prove unless one of our vice
presidents was glued to the keyhole of the loan representative's bedroom.

But the kickbacks on top of the seduction charges were
just too much. What this man had been doing was extracting
$20 or $30 each time he made a loan, telling the applicant

that the money would "help speed things along." What do the people know? If the average citizen has to pay a kid a buck or two to watch his car while going to eat dinner in an exotic part of town, he is going to take it for granted that on a $3,000 loan it might take $20 to get the deal moving.

One of the easiest ways to get conned is at that terrible time when you've struggled to pay off two-thirds of the loan and you've simply run out of money. So you trot into the bank and ask for a renewal, or another $2,000 on the loan. You point out that you've been an ace customer so far, paying back the bank on the dot every month, but the bidet has overflowed, ruining three rooms of your apartment and the place needs painting, flooring, tiling, etc. (And a new bidet.) Technically it's quite easy to get an extension because you've already passed the credit check hurdle, the interview, the bank's private and confidential evaluation of you as a customer. And of course you've been paying us back. The loan rep has a very easy time in deciding whether to give you a loan renewal: it's almost automatic under the circumstances I've described.

But the poor devil who is in hock to us generally doesn't realize this. He thinks he's going to have to sweat it out all over again. Romeo, the officer whom we nailed for kickbacks and free love, made it a specialty to hype individuals who were asking for renewals. He would size up the desperation of each case and then, because he was good enough to work out of the Actor's Studio, he would grimly shake his head and mutter something about paperwork and logjams and say maybe a week or ten days if the moon was right.

The man whose apartment is floating away right before

his eyes knows that he'll be living in Wilkes Barre, Pennsylvania, before that loan comes through and thus when the guy implies that a fast fifty might well smooth the tracks he figures what the hell. And that's how we grabbed Romeo.

It takes a mighty lapse in behavior for us to discharge one of our people. Romeo's case was such a lapse. But we couldn't prosecute because (1) we didn't have any physical evidence, and (2) even if we did, we wouldn't go to court. We'd be the laughingstock of the banking world if other bankers found out one of our loan reps was sleeping on the job, as it were. We simply fired Romeo and I'm sure he's cheerfully processing loans at another bank right this moment.

Now you might think after reading about all of the things we do to insure that our loans get repaid that we're in Fat City, with thousands of customers stopping by once a month to pay us back for their cars, boats, kids, ad infinitum. Not so. Depending on whether we're getting fleeced by the Penn Central or by some guy who bought a Volkswagen and left town, the amount of money lost on bad loans is staggering. In 1969, for instance, the six largest banks in New York City charged off $39 million in bad loans. That's all of the sharpies at Chase Manhattan, First National City, Manufacturers Hanover Trust, Morgan Guaranty Trust, Bankers Trust and Chemical New York. If 1969 was a good year for ripping off banks, 1970 was a banner year: that $39 million rose precipitously to $166 million!

In 1972, I'm proud to say, good old First Mutual Trust was right in the middle of the list in writing off bad loans. We even came close to Chase, a rather dubious distinction. We hurriedly put together a credit coordinating committee to review weekly any loans outstanding which are more than $750,000. This means that each week the committee meets, and in some cases when they go over the list of loans the question asked is as simple as, "Are they still in business?"

All of this is panic banking, instituting checks and procedures which obviously should have been in operation for years. But, just as we're one of the leaders in bad loans, so are we one of the leaders in antiquated procedures. Another problem about our starting this committee is that we may well have been four years too late. The Federal Reserve has laid down a 1 percent allowance for writing off bad loans as losses. Let us say, for example, that over a five-year period a bank has an average of $10 million of outstanding loans for every year. Let us also say your bad loan loss over a five-year period averages out to $100,000 a year, or 1 percent a year. Under accounting regulations, your bank is allowed to write 1 percent against income — and not a cent more. Fair enough, you say, and it is fair enough unless the economy goes to hell in any given period. Then there is chaos. Because, if your losses ever go above the formulated 1 percent a year, regulations prohibit your writing off anything above that mythical 1 percent. Let us say that in the fifth year your bad loans jumped to $120,000, and your outstanding loans remained constant. You can only write off the same $100,000 loss. Three and four years ago, banks were handing out money to companies and individuals with reckless abandon. When the market fell apart in 1969 and 1970 and when businesses started going to the wall, people and companies started defaulting on loans. And there are the regulations staring you in the face: you can only write off 1 percent — not 1¼ percent, not 1½ percent, but only 1 percent. When the outstanding losses soar, the writeoff stops at 1 percent, down go the net earnings, down goes the price of the stock, and out to Palm Springs goes the chairman.

There's nothing a bank can do when the Penn Central or the New Haven (an earlier disaster which foreshadowed the Penn Central disaster) go bad. Oh, I suppose we could go out and commandeer a few freight cars, but that's silly. When an individual tries to stiff us, we go after him. The law prohibits your garnisheeing a man's salary, but you can try for his assets.

We will write off loans if the balance of the loan is less than $25. We will write off a loan where the balance is between $26 and $51 if we haven't received any payment in two years. We give up if the individual goes into bankruptcy and there don't seem to be any visible assets. Obviously, if we smell a fraud, we hang in like tigers to get even a penny on the dollar. If you're in hock to us and you die and you had no estate, we tend not to go after your impoverished widow — we write you off. If you've borrowed from us and driven away in what amounts to our car, we will chase the hell out of you for six years, but then we give up. (By that time, your car/our money will have deteriorated/depreciated to nothing anyhow.) If we were stupid enough to lend you money when you were sixty-three and two years later you ended up retired and broke, we'll let you alone. (We're not all that nice; if we find you've got children who are still earning a living, we'll badger them to pay the loan off.) With apologies to Women's Liberation, if you're a housewife and you haven't paid us a penny in six years, we'll write you off. (And, needless to say, if you come to us as a housewife in the first place, the odds are we wouldn't have given you a loan because you were a housewife.)

If you've become permanently crippled or disabled and have been unable to work for a period of three years, we give up. And finally, if the pace of the twentieth century gets to be a little too much and you crack up, we will write your loan off but of course there's a slight catch: you have to have been crazy for at least three years, and that's being confined crazy, not your normal run-of-the-mill walking-around-on-the-outside crazy.

It goes without saying that you've got no estate worth attaching while you're being crazy. However, being crazy is not the easy way out you might think it is. If, for example, you go certifiably crazy and are confined to Valium Village for two and a half years and are let out, why, by golly we'll come after you and hound you for the rest of the loan. And don't tell us about any halfway house, either. What usually happens in the case of those who are insane and are then let go before three years are up is, we will do the definitive job of really driving them crazy and right back where they came from.

The Tony Corallosteins of our bank, having been conditioned by hounding ghetto residents for finance companies, are the resident experts at tracking down skips. ("Skips" is the all-encompassing generic term given to all those indebted to the bank who leave the vicinity.) And you can see that when we are talking about more than $26 and less than $51 we are talking about Tony. We have no procedure whatsoever when a Four Seasons Nursing Home dissolves right before our eyes, or when a National Student Marketing or a Commonwealth United suddenly disappears from view. Then (and the loan might be into the millions) we stand in line along with all the other creditors and try to get something back for our money. The faceless corporation fares infinitely better than the poor devil who cracks up owing us $1,500. The courts sanction our attitude toward the individual, no matter how small; the courts have yet to figure out how we get our millions back except to appoint a referee and try to solve a million dollar bust.

I don't want to give the impression that whenever an installment loan representative gets larcenous it's simply the nickel and dime variety, it's just not so. A Chase Manhattan branch out in Queens caught one of their loan officers whom I'll call Herman, in a scheme that cost the bank $44,000 before they got wise to him. Herman was a loan interviewer. He would sign loan papers, mostly automobile and home improvement loans. Herman had invented the following fictitious borrowers for Chase's hard-earned money: Edward Eckman, Richard Hutson, Arthur Carp, John Griffin, Harry Jacobs, Stanley Pell, Joe Brown, George Fay, John Finn, William Lee, William Stall, Vincent Lindsay, Harry Ganning, Peter Slovan, Frank Monroe, Charles Masler, Robert Graphy, John Hood, Walter Falman, and Joseph Moore. Twenty borrowers in all, and each loan just a bit over $2,000, and stupidly, each borrower with the same business address — a distributing company with a Babylon, Long Island, post office box. Even more stupidly, each loan was recommended by Herman.

On the twenty-first loan they caught up with Herman. Because none of the borrowers was particularly friendly with Chase, none was making the slightest move to pay back the loan to the bank. A collection gorilla who could read noticed that on two of his dunning jobs the man recommending the loan was Herman. Since the collection gorillas hang out together and since they have a natural tendency to talk shop, one gorilla mentioned casually to another that he had two bummers with Herman as a reference, and wasn't that strange? The second gorilla put down his banana long enough to say, gee, wasn't that curious, he too had a couple of deadbeat loans he was trying to collect on, and they too were Herman's doings. When a third collection gorilla chimed in that he had a Herman loan as well, someone higher up than the gorillas put two and two together and came up with the twenty phony loans. Herman was fired, naturally, and I don't know whether there was any prosecution or not. Herman told Chase that he used the money to go into the dry food mix business. I've talked to a number of people and they don't have the slightest idea of what dry food mixes are, and maybe that's why Herman went to hell in a basket with his business and needed all those loans.

First Mutual Trust has not been without its larger loan department scandals. The sweetest scheme I've heard of to date involved our old friends in the M*f*a. It seems that a real estate broker named Morris had been doing a lot of business for many years with one of our branch offices. Morris took out loans, his nephew Monroe took out loans, everyone in Morris's family took out loans from us. They were all properly secured and all approved by the branch manager. Unfortunately for us, Morris had a friend who had best be called Vinnie. Morris introduced Vinnie to his friendly branch manager and wouldn't you know it? Vinnie took out some loans.

Time passes and two things happened. The loan applications started getting sloppier: there weren't the proper loan division endorsements on them and they weren't properly secured. The other thing was that Morris and Vinnie had friends who were taking out some of these sloppy loans: a loan here to Angelo, there to Izzy, now a loan to a deceased brother-in-law of Morris, named Manny. The loans kept flowing and Morris and Vinnie kept bringing their friends around until one day the State of New York was holding an investigation into the loan sharking activities of the M*f*a, and whose name should turn up but Vinnie's? In fact, Vinnie's name was mentioned prominently in the hearings and one of the gumshoes from our collection division heard it and then (fortunately for us) remembered that Vinnie was a customer of ours.

When the cloud burst, we found sixty delinquent loans. We also found that some of our official proceeds checks (our loan money) showed forged signatures. Out of the sixty loan applications, only a handful were properly secured, properly signed, properly approved by the bank.

We then entered into a terribly involved negotiation with Morris to get some of our money back. Morris, like a true First Mutual Trust customer, was aghast that Vinnie should be using the proceeds of his loans to lend out the money at usurious rates. Shocking! He liquidated many of the loans, sold some of his stock in a rival bank of ours to pay off others, and then worked out a thirty-six-month plan to pay us back part of the $170,000 which went astray. We wrote off $45,000, giving the auditing office a busy few days to find a place to hide the loss.

And what about the branch manager? That's an interesting story in itself. We took his branch away from him (the ceremony is a bit less flamboyant than the cashiering of an officer from the army). We made him a floating branch manager, we kept the story out of the papers, we never gave the manager any key more significant than one to the men's room. And we hung a sign around his neck which said, "I will never approve a loan to any customer who is named Morris and who happens to have a friend named Vinnie and who also has a deceased brother-in-law named Manny."

# CHAPTER VI

THE profit margins in banks are smaller than in most enterprises — although food chains operate on a very low margin of profit, as do retail stores. The reasons for the low margins in banks are quite evident: a bank deals basically in what is called, around race tracks, "vigorish." Let us say that you decide to bet on a football game — although that is an illegal activity — and you wager $50 on your team to win. Your team wins, you collect $50. Well and good. But if your team loses, you owe the man on the other end of the bookie's telephone $55 — that $5 or 10 percent being the vigorish.

We operate much the same way, and we've got vigorish, too, but not as juicy as 10 percent. Our percentage runs no more than 3 to 3½ percent. If you are dumb enough to keep your savings in one of our savings accounts, we'll pay you (as of early 1973) 4½ percent interest, but if you stroll in and ask for a loan, we'll get around 7½ percent interest back from you. That vagrant 3 percent is our vigorish and it has to pay for a lot of rent, salaries, medical benefits, film for our cameras which will spot you if you try to rob us, guns (without bullets) for our guards, and so forth. Pure upkeep, as the money flows back and forth.

But, as you can see, banks do occasionally make bad

loans, lose money, get caught in bad markets, foul up trust funds, and simply fritter money away in a thousand different ways. And the people who run banks, watching the industries they help finance develop new products, sometimes get caught up in what could be called the Edsel complex (after the beauty that the Ford Motor Company saddled us with). The notion which almost sunk First Mutual Trust Company was the credit card craze which swept the world (and the bankers along with it) six years ago. It is a lovely case study in foolishness, greed, stupidity, avarice, and dumbo banking.

Credit cards sponsored by banks originated, along with all of the other cuckoo notions, out in California, when the Bank of America issued a credit card called BankAmericard. A nice name, redolent of flags waving in a sea of greenbacks.

Now banks are competitive in the eyes of the potential customer, whose eyes we hope are glued to our advertising on television. But internally, structurally, and in management function most banks are extremely similar. Except for California. The California banks — again, our friends at Bank of America — were decades ahead of the eastern banks in financing movies. And in credit cards.

When the Bank of America sprung the BankAmericard on the public (scaring the wits out of Diners Club and American Express), we eastern bankers immediately took a look, a very close look, westward. There is a network — or practically a buddy system — among bankers. What we do is find a typical model of our bank — in a progressive state like California — and then one of our astronauts flies out and spends some time with his friends at Bank of America or wherever, checking out their new system. In the counterculture this is called ripping off. In banking it's called the study of existing modular systems. So much for semantics.

The astronaut we picked for the investigation of the California credit card was a man named Oswald, who was of the right religion, color, college background, connections. He had come to us from another large New York bank and he was out to make his mark as a comer in the organization. No sooner did Oswald hear of BankAmericard than he was winging westward. We got an occasional postcard from him — he said the St. Francis Hotel was terrific, but their wine cellar was a little weak Bordeauxwise. He chalked up that limitation to the jingoistic attitude of Californians toward Almaden and other local grapes. Not one word about BankAmericard, except to say that the system developed at Bank of America certainly seemed viable. Because Oswald didn't want to leave any stone unturned, he zipped down to Los Angeles for a short stop at the Beverly Hills Hotel. Not one word about the credit card business in Los Angeles, just a bit of carping about the tourists in the Polo Lounge.

The first thing Oswald did upon returning was to work out an involved study on the feasibility of our getting into the credit card business. We took into account the costs of the various card alternatives, the financial projections of startup costs, initial losses, date of turnaround from loss to profitability, pertinent share of market statistics, a description of proposed services, management requirements. The whole thing. The study said there were three ways to get into the business:

(*1*) We could take a compatible plan from someone else's credit card operation and start our own. (In some circles this is called stealing.)

(2) We could enter into a licensing agreement with an existing credit card (such as BankAmericard).

(3) We could start our own plan from scratch.

It was a marvelous study and Oswald made a brilliant presentation to the executive committee of the bank. He forgot only one thing in his report. We at First Mutual Trust knew not one thing about the credit card business, or the mail order business (by which members are solicited), and very little about the retail business in the city of New York. But aside from these minor drawbacks, we were ready to roll.

On top of that we were greedy as hell. We figured option (2) meant our millions of projected profits would have to be shared, and we couldn't stomach the thought of that. We thought about (3) but we really didn't know where to start, so we opted for (1), which was stealing.

One of the things that Oswald carried back to New York was the complete marketing plan for a California operation, and I hasten to add that it wasn't the Bank of America's. We then took their figures and projected them for New York. The California bank reported that the three major cost elements involved — developing the system, getting people in, and first-year operating costs — were indeed heavy, but within one year the money would be rolling in so fast we couldn't count it.

In 1969, when we were about to launch the First Mutual Trust Company's "Easy Buck Card," the other New York banks were also cranking up to enter the sweepstakes. I shouldn't leave the reader with the impression that we were the only bank struck with swamp fever: we all had it. First National City turned out something called the Everything Card and then changed the name of it and joined the Master Charge Card system. Chase Manhattan started the Unicard and for reasons best known to Chase eventually switched to BankAmericard. Bankers Trust Company began with the Check Guarantee Card and moved on to BankAmericard. Manufacturers Hanover, Chemical Bank, Franklin National all took on Master Charge, while the Bank of Commerce, the National Bank of North America, and the Security National Bank joined BankAmericard. Greed City again.

The fatal error in our Easy Buck Card was charmingly simple: Oswald the astronaut had done all of his numbers based on a California bank and then had simply said that the California numbers would hold up for New York, except that they might be a bit higher. He estimated that in our first year the operating losses would be $1,500,000. Things were going along swimmingly in 1970 until an auditor literally died in a sea of red ink. After one full year we had income of $8,500,000, which was nice, but we had expenses of $12,000,000. You will note that the difference between the estimated loss and the real loss of $3,500,000 is only $2,000,000. Now if one of our junior officers had committed a blunder in which the bank got stiffed for $2,000, his career would be in jeopardy. But Oswald, destined for greatness, hung in like a champ.

If 1970 was a disaster, 1971 was in some ways worse. The income remained about the same — $8,500,000 — but the expenses went up another $1,000,000. Well, here we are two years in the hopper, and about $8 million absolutely out the window. And although you may blithely talk to your Board of Directors and say the $8 million "can be written off," that money has still fled the coop. With $8 million lying around, we could have had every employee's teeth capped so we would be the smiling bank.

Nineteen seventy-two was supposed to be the break-even year and 1972 was also the year we put the lid on any information coming out of the credit card division. I was told by one survivor of the debacle that still another $1,500,000 went down the tubes.

If you're morbidly curious as to exactly where the first year's $12,000,000 of yearly expenses occur, listen to how one of the nation's leading banks pissed away its money. About $3,000,000 went to salaries; another $300,000 went to overtime because no one (except Oswald) knew the systems or how they worked; agency help, $300,000; employee benefits, $300,000; rental space, $750,000; furniture and equipment, $600,000; advertising, $600,000; stationery and supplies (all those direct mail pieces), $1,500,000; telephone and telegraph, $500,000; travel and entertainment, $100,000; postage, $525,000; consultants' fees (the experts who were brought in to bail us out), $385,000. Now that staggering amount of money doesn't add up to $12,-000,000, but I forgot to add what Oswald forgot to project correctly: fraud — what every New Yorker has a little bit of in his heart and soul. In that first year of operation, fraud ran us close to $3,500,000. And that, folks, is one hell of a lot of fraud.

All of our projections had been based on what I'll have to call the Sunshine Bank of California, a sunny outfit with assets about the same as ours, and in many ways *our* bank. Except, of course, that they had more sense at Sunshine than we did. Sunshine of California had first-year losses of $1,200,000 — and when Oswald took their figures and made his extrapolation, he added on another $300,000 just to make sure. Things cost more in New York, was his reasoning. In the second year of Sunshine's operation they showed a loss on the books of $27,000, which in an operation like a credit card is just about breaking even. The third year of operation at Sunshine was another Gold Rush, with money crawling out of the walls.

Oswald was a clever fellow, and actually before we launched Easy Buck we even went to the trouble of checking out a conservative eastern bank — Old Revolutionary Bank of Philadelphia. Their card — called Minuteman Money — was also successful and their numbers were similar to Sunshine's of California. The one factor which everyone agreed would be higher here than in California or Philadelphia was the cost of advertising.

Oswald was very much in evidence the first six months or so of our operation. For one thing, he had a hand in designing the card. We hired an artist whose work was astonishingly similar to that of the artist Peter Max, and the product was a silver card with an overflowing cornucopia in the center. Need I say that spilling out of the cornucopia was money? And Oswald was pushing for an early start: every week or so he'd come in and say that he'd heard that First National City was about to launch their Everything Card; or Chase was moving right along with BankAmericard. He kept pushing, and in pushing overlooked a crucial point: both the California bank and the Philadelphia bank had done very careful homework on their cards before launching them. Both banks had hired expert mail order people; both banks knew of the danger lurking in mail order lists which had not been verified or "cleaned" of deadbeats. But not Oswald or First Mutual Trust.

Out our cards went, with the name of the bank barely dry on the card itself. We sent out thousands, hundreds of thousands, perhaps millions. We had an orgy of mailing; we papered the city of New York with our cards. We also, using the good name of First Mutual Trust Company, signed up every good, bad or indifferent retail establishment to be a participating merchant. We're all going to get rich, was our siren song. You didn't have to apply for our card; we just sent the thing to you and as soon as you signed it, away you went. Oh, you did fill in an application at the same time you received the card and you mailed that back to us for a routine credit check. But meanwhile, be our guest. Buy, buy, buy, the good old American way.

During that first fiscal year of 1970, the fraud losses started slowly. In January of 1970, with the glut of cards just reaching the customers, there wasn't any fraud. February was quiet, too. March of 1970 showed $10,000 of fraud and there was cheering in the bank — we had built into the first-year budget a fraud figure and the first quarter figures (only $10,000) were astonishingly low. Oswald quit buying his clothes at Barney's and switched to Dunhill Tailors, where our chairman suited up.

In April fraud suddenly jumped to $100,000, in May it dipped to $81,000, in June it climbed back to $109,000 and July and August also showed $100,000 for each month. The planners were revising their budgets and Oswald was looking a little peaked — natty in his Dunhill suit, but peaked nonetheless. What we didn't realize, of course, was that the worst was yet to come. September brought us a fraud figure of $1 million. There were two heart attacks in the credit card division, eight ulcers, three nervous breakdowns, and Oswald discovered that Dunhill's wouldn't take back his $450 suit.

October, November, and December each had losses of about $700,000 and there was hysteria in the bank. Our earnings were shot to hell, the chairman canceled weekends in Palm Springs and heads were about to roll. Even though the money was flowing out of the bank like a — well, like a cornucopia — one hand didn't let the other hand know what was going on. The promotion people were still busily mailing out cards to (it turned out later) just about everyone on the voter registration lists. The only problem was that although the names might have been voting from cemeteries, they turned out to be very active when it came to buying.

The premise of all bank credit card operations is that you can walk into a store like Korvette's in New York, which is a very large discount/department store, buy $500 worth of appliances, give them your Easy Money card, and walk off with the merchandise. Because you used your card to buy the merchandise, rather than cash, the assumption is that you were subtly encouraged to buy — perhaps more than you normally would have had you used cash. For this privilege Korvette's gives up a few points — percentage points — and this is called the merchant's discount. During our disaster, the merchant's discount was running about 3 percent. This means at the end of the month, when Korvette's sent us your $500 bill, we paid them $485 immediately — the bill less the merchant's discount. This was fine with Korvette's, because they didn't have the headache of collecting the bill; we did. And Korvette's got their money right on the button; that's another premise of the credit card system.

So there we were, pouring out millions of dollars to reputable department stores like Korvette's and then discovering that the people who had used our cards to charge the appliances might just as well have been buried in a cemetery. If you recall the grim World War II movie about the man who is taken by the Nazis and all letters addressed to him are returned with the notation "Address Unknown," you now will understand why we began calling our credit card operation "Address Unknown." In our haste to blanket the city with cards, and with no control of either identification or credit, we discovered to our horror that Bowery bums were zipping around town with our cards, charging up a storm, and then disappearing to the Bowery, to laugh their hearts out. It's lucky that you can't charge booze on a credit card or our losses would have doubled.

One of the worst things we did was to mail the goddam cards to our own customers repeatedly, with a strident pitch to get out there in the marketplace and buy. Some of our customers shrugged the first time the free card arrived in the mail; others got mildly unhappy on the second card arriving; and many, many others took the third card, and the fourth, and just scattered them to the wind. I know of one girl who got seven of the damned things and she gaily gave them to her out-of-work and deadbeat friends. Although the friends didn't quite understand what it was all about, they knew enough to sign her name on the cards and charge away.

As the tons of bills began to flood in from the department stores, our system was nonoperative; actually, we had no system. There are witnesses who will swear in a court of law that at the beginning the incoming bills from retailers were kept in a cigar box. (We later switched to three cigar boxes.) When I heard that, I knew we all ought to head for the hills. Ma and Pa delicatessens have better ways of accounting than to keep their bills in a cigar box.

Keeping their eyes on the cigar boxes were 35 officers and 354 in clerical help. We had loads of staff during the disaster: we had an administration unit, an operations group, a marketing section, a collection group, a credit card security group, and three cigar boxes. Interestingly, we didn't have the credit card division in our main headquarters: we found some ratty space uptown, shoved the 389 people into the space, and then avoided the division like the plague. Oswald never went near it; he always seemed to have work at his desk during lunch hour.

What I haven't mentioned in this tidal wave of disaster is that we launched the credit card in the depths of a depression. Call 1969 to 1971 a Nixon recession, call it a downswing in the economy, I'll call it an honest-to-God depression. Any banker can tell you that it was. And our marketing people, in starting up the Easy Buck Card, forgot that during a depression and/or recession, consumers of every economic level have a tendency not to pay their bills with the regularity that they normally do. Ask any dentist or doctor about bill collection during a depression, and he will tell you.

People in New York and the rest of the United States were not paying their bills on time to Macy's, Gimbel's, Korvette's, or anybody during that period. Here we come with, as we called it, a "new form of money," and the people lapped it up. A new way to charge, a new set of people to stiff. Customers who would let their department store bill lag for two months felt with our card that, what the hell, let it slide for four months. Who's to tell? And, if we had sent them not one card but *four,* they would instinctively say to each other, "My God, if the banks are so fouled up that they're sending out four cards, let's not even pay the bill; maybe they'll be so mixed up that they'll forget the bill, too." Logical and sound thinking, and this attitude on the part of the cardholders brought forth a specter of such horror that our people had blocked it away entirely. The specter was something called laughingly "the cost of funds."

If a bank lends you money, they've got to get it from somewhere. Either they have to take it out of their working capital or borrow it from somebody else so you can have your money. Banks stay afloat because, hopefully, they are using their money to the fullest every minute of the day. A banker's mind dictates that every dollar in his bank should be earning interest for him somehow, someway. At the outset, as I said, we had a gross income of $8.5 million and expenses of $12 million, a net loss of $3.5 million, which is a loss of such magnitude that you just can't sweep it into the miscellany category in your annual report. But what I didn't add into that net loss, and what the bank didn't tell its stockholders, was that the actual loss to the bank was much more. The *cost of funds* more than doubled our loss the first year.

At the end of our first full operational year, 1970, we had made cash advances of $16 million and $41 million in delayed payments. In plain English, we already had paid the Korvettes of this world $16 million on receipt of their bills. They had given out the goods and they wanted their money. What we were trying to do was collect on $41 million owed to us by our customers, customers who were trying to defraud us by not paying at all, customers who were dragging their feet, customers who had flown to Mexico, charging it to us.

Forty-one million dollars in delayed payments is a little higher than the average we settled into. At any given moment during the credit card program — that is, if you were to say, "What is going on as of February 1?" — the average cash advance would be about $12 million and delayed payments would be $29 million. Add those up and you should get $41 million; the factor that First Mutual Trust built into such equations was: if we had that $41 million out on the streets working for us, we should be making 9 percent interest. Multiply 9 percent times $41 million and give or take a hundred thousand, you've got about $3.7 million in the cost of funds — lost interest never to be recovered. Add the cost of funds to the actual loss of the program and that first full year really cost us over $7 million. Plus the cigar boxes.

When disasters of this style hit any bank, bodies start to run and heads start to roll. In the first 15 months of operation we ran through four chief officers of the credit card division. You would have thought that with this kind of financial drain the bank would have sent in their top troubleshooters. Well, they did, in a fashion. One of the troubleshooters cracked up and simply quit talking. We thought he was just a quiet type until his secretary mentioned to someone in personnel that he hadn't talked to her for three weeks. That's shell shock, and off he was carted. Another of our ace troubleshooters who had built his reputation on headaches walked in, took one look, and suddenly had his wife develop a near-fatal disease. He told the president of the bank he was with us all the way, but he had to sit home and hold his wife's hand and he didn't think he'd have the time to try and sort out the credit card operation. There's not much that the president can do when an officer pleads terminal illness of a close relative. (I think, though, that the president would have drawn the line at a first cousin.) When the wife recovered splendidly months later from whatever she was stricken with, just about everyone had forgotten that the officer had used her as an excuse.

The third troubleshooter we brought in was supposedly an expert who knew everything there was to know about credit cards and computers — a fairly essential combination because a clean credit card operation depends on a smoothly functioning computer. The expert was brilliant but couldn't talk English: He only knew how to speak in various computer tongues, and although that's all right, I suppose, he was unable to translate the problems for the management who couldn't speak computerese. It was at this point that the guy who started it all, Oswald the astronaut, pulled off a very nifty move. (I should interject that banks, like all organizations, are very political, and the higher up the corporate ladder you go, the more intricate the office politics become.) Oswald had been setting his sights on a job in charge of marketing. So Oswald suggested to the president that perhaps the man to bail out the credit card tangle was the marketing man, Ewald. Ewald it was, and he lasted no more than two or three months, staying long enough to put a permanent black mark on his record and leaving the door in the marketing division wide open for Oswald to creep in.

As the credit card mess deepened, Oswald naturally kept pulling farther and farther away from it, until two years after he had written his original proposal most people had forgotten he had had anything to do with it. (Had the operation turned into a booming success, Oswald would have been right in there claiming credit, which is the company way of doing things.)

Instead of looking for administrative talent to straighten

out things, the bank tried to lose interest in the operation; they started using the credit card division as the Siberia of the bank for senior officers. Why the very top management started to take this attitude is beyond me but they did, and in doing so came damned close to toppling the bank. The first of the misfits they tossed into the maw was a man named Hathaway, who became befuddled at the sight of $3.5 million in fraud. After a succession of Hathaways, in a desperation move, the bank found a young man in the installment loan division who knew something about credit, something about customer service, and handed him the mess.

The young man, an unheralded nonastronaut named Rosenberg, managed in a few months to get expenses under a semblance of control and he also was able to convince the top management that they had to start building into the budget a realistic figure for fraud. Previously, management had been trying to evade the facts of life — and assumed there could be no fraud in the city of New York.

The problem that we now faced — and all banks always face — is how much truth we were going to tell each other and our stockholders. Or our board of directors. I wasn't present when the chairman winged in from California and had to explain to the board that the reason the 1970 earnings were shot to hell was because of the credit card fiasco. But I did read how we officially finessed it in the annual report which was issued in 1971. We said, in effect, that the entire banking industry was moving to the "checkless society." One of the ways, said our report, of entering the checkless society was through bank-owned and-operated credit cards; so although we were experiencing considerable startup costs, it was going to be worth it because, after all, the checkless society was what American life was all about, wasn't it? What the annual report didn't say was that it was going to cost the stockholders $7 million in earnings.

All companies work on plans; banks, especially. In a plan-oriented environment, groups, divisions (and you could say battalions) submit plans some six months ahead of actuality, or real time. The 1974 budgets are put together in 1973; the plans for operational expenses and potential profits are calculated in the quiet summer months and must be approved up and down the executive level. What happened to the Easy Buck Card was that it was programmed into all of the 1969 and 1970 plans, and is to this day calculated very carefully. But what wasn't fed into the plans for a year and a half was the cost of funds and the potential loss due to fraud.

One lie fed another, and when the guys running the credit card operation saw their ship about to go down, they turned to consultants — about $500,000 worth the first year. The consultants breezed into our offices with an awful lot of confidence, and even the cigar boxes didn't shake them too much. They've got their interests to protect, and they're not going to sit there and tell us to get out of the credit card business, take our loss like gentlemen, and stick to banking. It is to their self-interest to keep us in the credit card business, not get us out of it. The consultants kept fiddling with the numbers and the best that they could do was to say that fraud would probably remain constant at $2 million, expenses would probably stay at their same level, but our collection rate might increase.

What nobody has ever said during the incredible four years we've been in this business is that we're in a business outside of our areas of expertise. Banking is thoroughly regulated; our rates are the same as anyone else's in town. The credit card business is not formally regulated by the government, and we were innocents in the grownup world of business. Nobody to my knowledge breathed the words American Express during any of the carrying on with the Easy Buck Card.

Now the people at American Express are not dummies. (Well, they were taken rather grandly in a wonderful salad oil swindle, but that was years ago and even Tino DeAngelis has been released from the kip and says he'll never touch a drop of salad oil for the rest of his life.) While all of the Mickey Mouse banks were fooling around with credit cards, Big Daddy American Express was gearing up its operation, too, and it is my humble opinion that American Express will eventually knock out all of the bank credit cards.

You'll note that in the past four years what was a fairly restricted credit card used mostly in restaurants has been considerably broadened to include every airline in the world (thus knocking the stuffings out of the vaunted Air Travel Card), every hotel worth sleeping in in the world, and now they've set their sights on retail establishments. Witness Macy's in New York, Harrods in London, Tiffany's, and so forth. American Express has a lot of muscle, a lot of expertise, and considerably more knowledge in credit card checking and promotion than any bank has.

The retail establishments themselves are not foolish either: Korvette's would rather push its own credit card than our credit card. They save the 3 or 4 percent and they can program their credit card into their own accounting operation without any great difficulty. As for restaurants, the smartest of the restaurants in New York refuse to take any credit cards. If you don't happen to have any cash on you, they'll open a charge account for you right on the spot. What they're trying to avoid is paying the 7 percent or so they have to fork over to American Express every time a meal is charged.

And so the earnings of the bank suddenly dropped over a dollar a share and the chill of disaster could be felt among the security analysts who watched over bank stocks. We could — and did — tell the security analysts, "Our credit card approach continues to make satisfactory progress according to the increases in the volume of business, the number of active card holders and total retail outlets that will accept the card. It is anticipated that in the near future the program will be contributing substantially to net earnings." But who would believe us?

What will happen with our card? Well, I suppose we'll eventually figure out how to cut down on the fraud and we'll eventually get the expenses into line and perhaps we'll learn how to collect better. But it's going to take time. Meanwhile, the losses plus the cost of funds keep mounting. Adding net losses to loss due to cost of funds, I'd say that we've got pretty close to $11 million down the drain so far.

The impact the losses had on the bank were felt in many ways. We pulled in our horns everywhere. We almost got out of home mortgages completely; we got out of construction loans; we laid off everything we could that would require cash on the line. When we should have been expanding our retail division, we didn't; when we should have been expanding our international division, we took a look at the increasing competition and practically went out of international banking; when we should have been thinking about our role in the deteriorating central city, we weren't. In short, we were utterly consumed with and by the credit card. And we were not alone, and our problems were not unique either.

Obviously I don't know what the other banks are doing with their cards, but I somehow doubt that anyone is making the millions they thought they would when they began. Although we might be run a little lousier than most banks, even the best-run bank is out of its league in the credit card business. The best that we can hope for — now that we're hooked as deeply as we are — is that eventually we'll get the system running as best it can and perhaps it will turn a profit. I doubt it will ever earn back what went into it. Nor can we simply say casually one day, "Folks, we've decided to get out of the credit card business." Because if we did, we'd have to turn around and write off all those losses and then explain to the board and the general stockholders what the hell went wrong.

Although I spent quite a bit of time talking to people about the Easy Buck Card, I never could get them to admit my pet theory regarding our disaster: to wit, that the California bank we stole from just might have fed us phony figures. Perhaps, just perhaps, the Sunshine Bank of California took a terrible beating that first year and instead of losing $1.2 million, which they said they did, maybe their losses ran above $3 million, the way ours did. And maybe they didn't break even the second year. Maybe they took a bath too. It might be possible that they were too embarrassed about their losses to give us the real picture. I only know that the smartest operators in the bank knocked a dollar off our stock's earnings with "Easy Buck," and it will be years before we recover from the beating.

# CHAPTER VII

I N early 1972, the *New York Times* ran an interesting piece about Chemical New York's "street banking" program. They've opened up a branch in the heart of Harlem and staffed it with young and sympathetic officers who can speak the language of the streets, thus the name of the program. The banker the piece focused on implied that he was out on 125th Street every day slinging the lingo around, like, man, come and dig our bank and put some of your bread in it, or truck on out with some of it. I liked the story and I liked Chemical's attempt to do business in Harlem.

No more than three weeks later, also in the *Times,* there was a news story describing the attempts being made by Chemical to shut one of their branches on Columbus Avenue and Eighty-first Street. Chemical was pretty nice about it, but the *Times* pointed out that you took your life in your hands if you went out for a loaf of bread on Columbus and Eighty-first Street, much less brought a payroll into the bank.

But you just can't close down a branch. You must first get permission from the controller of currency in Washington, D.C., and then additional permission from your state banking department. If you are simply a state chartered bank, permission is required only from your state banking department. But both agencies are reluctant to allow banks to open and shut branches with abandon.

These two accounts of Chemical's woes illustrate some of the problems that banks have today in expanding their retail business. And, as central cities change radically all over the United States, this simply isn't a problem restricted to New York. It is being duplicated in Los Angeles, Philadelphia, Detroit, Cleveland. And in Europe as well. People become more affluent, they move to better housing, which in many cases is out of the central core.

The leaders in New York City banking — in the branch race — are First National City and Chase Manhattan. As of this writing, First National City has 223 branches and Chase 179 branches, but they're so competitive about opening new ones that the figures are very subject to change. First Mutual Trust has 126 branches, and our branch development and location division is run by a former farmer from Iowa named Hiram.

How we happened to have a farmer running branch location in the city of New York is, in itself, a strange story. It all started with Lance in personnel, who, as I remarked earlier, was an anomaly in banking; he was a vault queen. Lance had a lot of influence in the bank and gradually he recruited a few too many of his choicer pals. Also, management began to look at Lance's Lads a bit closer because they all were stunningly good-looking, perpetually tanned, impeccably turned out. They looked too perfect even for a bank, which demands cleanth to the nth degree.

One of Lance's last recruits was Hiram, tanned, good-looking, but, as I said, a farmer. Also, straight as a die, with a farm-girl wife and six children. The bank finally eased Lance out, politely but out, and reexamined every one of his recruits. Hiram was left locating branches after a senior vice president personally checked out the wife and six children. Lance left the bank willingly. He told himself that if he had been so wrong about the potential of Hiram, then he was losing his touch.

I ought to interject that when a banker refers to his bank he is usually referring to the entity as a whole: the entire corporate structure, with its international and national operations, its financing and investment capabilities, its strength in investment trust situations, its interests in real estate, and so on and so on. When the ordinary citizen says, "I've got to go to my bank," he usually is talking about his neighborhood branch. The customer sees the branch as the bank; the bank sees the branch as but one small segment of one division of the bank. Unfortunately, while thinking this way, too many bankers neglect the individual branch.

Although it seems so at times, branches of banks just don't open willy-nilly: there is supposed to be a rhyme and a reason to the whole thing. Branch location is a science, we are told continually, a study of demographics, urban population, foot and vehicular traffic, and many other factors. And we know that a good portion of the cash flow in a bank is generated by its branches: much of its working capital comes from all of those eager customers who want to have checking or savings accounts with us.

Before Hiram took over branch location division, the operation was run by one of our old-line Irishmen, Pat O'Connor, a rough-and-tumble operator who had been with the bank for almost forty years. O'Connor was given branch location after he had been booted out of the operations division. Pat did not trust computers, did not believe in them, and consequently we were almost the last bank in New York to switch to computer operations. When we finally did, it cost us a fortune to catch up with the other banks in sophistication and techniques. When Pat retired at age sixty-five, Hiram was given the job. Why, nobody knows. Hiram had a bit of knowledge in how to milk a cow, but he didn't know a damned thing about locating a branch of a bank.

But there is a set procedure in branch location and for the first few months Hiram went along with what his assistants told him was the proper drill. A bank like ours might open five or six new branches a year, and since this is a multimillion dollar business, each time out it's quite tricky.

As Hiram was assuming control we were charging full steam ahead with a branch in what was to be called the New Dodger Shopping Center, named for the departed Brooklyn Dodgers. This shopping center was a vast enterprise situated in Mill Basin, put together by some imaginative and, in the long run, stupid real estate promoters. Hiram, needless to say, had never been to Brooklyn, but he gave the plans a cursory okay and that was that. Officers in the division had gone to the site and had taken hundreds of photographs which showed the traffic in the area. They had gone to city hall and had done surveys on the automobile traffic in the neighborhood; they checked the police to find out the crime-rate growth in the Mill Basin neighborhood.

Yes, branch location is a diligent organization: they go to post offices in the area and find out how many eight-cent stamps are sold in a given week. I don't know what this has to do with the quality of your branch, but they count stamps. Likewise telephone calls. We pester the hell out of the telephone company to find out about message units and calls made from the area. We want to know about postal money orders bought in the area. We are insatiably curious to learn if the population is stable. (For "stable population" read: how many blacks have entered the area and how many whites have left it in the past ten years. If you think we are snoops before we hire an officer, or if we are nosy about your past before we lend you money, we really get bothersome before we build a branch.)

As I've said before, the problems are such that once you build a branch, there you are — stuck with the damned building. Not only won't the federal and/or state agencies let you casually off the hook, what can you do with a used two-story bank building? Not much, unless you open a government food store and use the vault to keep the cheese in. Banks these days cost $500,000 and up, depending on what the land is going to cost.

After branch location does its studies and photographs, a gigantic meeting is held with most of the top officers of the retail banking division, the administration division, a few stragglers from the executive committee, the real estate division, and the various regions of the bank which are involved. The photographs are spread out and the presentation is made. (Unfortunately, in the case of our Mill Basin branch, the original presentation had been made by Pat O'Connor, and since he had been raised in Brooklyn, everyone assumed Pat knew what he was talking about when he okayed the bank.) Then real estate takes over and starts the haggling over the land. Bids are let, hard hats with plans start moving into the area, and there we go.

So up went Mill Basin. Except we failed to do one thing: we never sent any engineers out to check the site. Since we were going into a shopping center with an established group of builders and developers, no one thought to check the site: they assumed the developers had. Well, the story is even more grisly than you can imagine. It turned out that the entire Mill Basin area was swamp covered with landfill (landfill in New York usually is garbage) and the New Dodger Shopping Center started to sink into the ground right after the first gentle spring rain. Our bank sank along with everything else. Hiram, newly in charge of branch location, got very hysterical, as well he might.

Unless you've been through it, you really can't comprehend what happens when a bank casually sinks into the ground several inches every year. But let me assure you, the problems inherent in such a sinking are immense. After every rain the basement of the bank was flooded. In severe rains, the water would rise out of the basement, which meant that the apricot carpeting which Hiram had agonized over got soaked. Apricot carpeting does not take water stains from landfill spillage very well. In fact, not at all. We replaced the carpeting in the bank on an average of four times a year. The draperies, hung with such care, were always damp and mildewed two feet from the bottom. We solved that by ordering draperies two feet shorter than normal.

After the first few disastrous rains, the home office got used to the panic-stricken calls from the New Dodger branch saying, "The water is into the teller area and onto the platform." (If the water had stayed in the teller area, we would have reacted eventually. But once it had the nerve to move over to the platform where the officers might get their toes wet, the mops were sent out immediately.) Naturally, the humorists in the bank began making jokes about the

Mill Basin disaster. "Instead of toasters, why don't we give out scuba masks and flippers?" one wit said.

To date, the branch — and the entire shopping center for that matter — has sunk about two and a half feet. That's our half million dollar branch going right down (excuse the expression) the drain.

The personal element in banking will rear its head in the damnedest places. For example, twelve management committees can do their homework on a million dollar mortgage loan, but at the highest level the decision to make or not to make the loan may depend on whether the chairman of the bank likes the way the chairman of the company applying for the loan plays golf. International loans have been known to come together or fall apart on the strength of the quality of wine at dinner. This human element creeps into bank location, too.

Take our branch in a small town in Nassau County, which is a heavily populated bedroom area right next to New York City. One of our senior vice presidents lived in the small town of Cedarhurst, a rather high income village, and many of his neighbors were officers at other New York banks. On the main street of Cedarhurst were branches of practically every bank in the city but ours, and this rankled our man. He felt slighted and inadequate. At Saturday night barbecues his neighbors would talk about their branch over on Main Street, but our man had nothing to say in return. So he began agitating for a branch to be built in Cedarhurst.

A squad of site experts went out to Cedarhurst and found it to be vastly overbuilt with banks: the town was lousy with them. What Cedarhurst did not need was another bank. No matter, the senior vice president kept pushing top management at First Mutual Trust, saying we were missing out on a vast new market to be tapped. The branch location people went back to Cedarhurst because this time Hiram had caved in to the various management pressures, instigated by the officer who lived in Cedarhurst. "For God's sake," Hiram said, "find a place to build a branch and let's be done with it."

In desperation, we found a plot of ground next to the railroad station in town. Main Street and the rest of the banks in Cedarhurst were blocks away, and the extent of potential customer traffic consisted of a newspaper shop, which sold hot coffee to commuters waiting for the Long Island Rail Road in the morning. As for a continual flow of pedestrian traffic, there wasn't any.

Up went the bank. It opened with a minimum of fanfare, and I think I can safely say that it is the only branch of a major New York bank right next to a railroad station. It does no business whatsoever. We lose a fortune on it every year, but it kept the senior vice president happy while he lived in Cedarhurst. Unfortunately, he only stayed in the town two years after the bank went up. He then proclaimed to one and all that "undesirables" were moving into his town, so he sold his house and moved to what he said was a fancier and better community. Our bank remains, a little lonely, but if you ever happen to take the Long Island Rail Road out to Cedarhurst you'll see us, next to Al's Newsstand.

The problems with branch location are immense, and they are further complicated by the fact that most of the management personnel, like Hiram, don't know too much about the city in which they transact their business.

We put up a sparkling branch in Queens. It had a terrific location, the land was cheap, the construction went off without a hitch, transportation was good, and Hiram got all spruced up for the traditional cocktail party the night before the opening. He got the shock of his life on his way into the bank that evening. One of our newer immigrants to New York City was idly standing by the bank watching all the comings and goings when Hiram drove up in one of our bank's limousines. He got out with a flourish, and as he started into the bank the bystander sidled up to him and said, "Listen, you gringo motherfucker, we don't want your capitalistic bank in our neighborhood." I happened to be standing nearby when this little byplay took place — Hiram's face went dead white. I don't think anyone in Iowa had ever called him a "gringo motherfucker"; perhaps he didn't know what it meant. But suddenly he did understand that something was terribly wrong with the bank. Indeed it was. We had put up a bank in an area that was changing from tortoni to tortillas, from pigs' knuckles to pigs' feet. Branch location failed to note that a number of the nearby stores carried mostly rice and red beans, and undoubtedly they knew not from the familiar sign "Bodega." In less than a year the neighborhood was entirely Spanish-speaking. We just weren't equipped to staff a bank with Spanish-speaking personnel, and naturally the bank was running in the red in a few months.

I suppose all of this would sound implausible if we were a small-time operation, but we aren't. We're a big bank. We even have a branch map room which is something out of *Dr. Strangelove*, except that it has large blowups of each borough of the city with various-colored pins designating our branches, along with our competitors'. Branch location is holed up in the map room for days on end and then we open a branch next to a Spanish church. This ignorance of the city and its people amounts to arrogance. We bankers go home to Westchester and shut our eyes as the Penn Central trains roar through the devastation in Harlem. We blindly assume that New York City is a friendly place, comprised of little neighborhood hamlets, somewhat on the order of Ridgefield, Connecticut. We do our research, we take our thousands of pictures, but we are remote from the people. When we open a branch, we give away pots, pans, electric toasters — just plain junk. And although the people flock to the openings and fight for the electric blankets, they don't come back and do a continual business with us.

Whenever branch location tried to get ethnic in their thinking, the results were almost worse than when we inadvertently made a mistake. We decided to tap the Jewish market out in one of the distant reaches of Far Rockaway, which is a section at the outer city limits. There was a beach near the location, a seedy boardwalk, and a dingy amusement park. But we felt that the heavily Jewish neighborhood would more than amply support our branch. What we should have figured out — but didn't — when we got the land for a steal, was that something was amiss. Indeed there was. The amusement park was about to go bankrupt. The crowds of people who used to flock to the park and the boardwalk in the summer, thus filling the coffers of the local businessmen, were no more. Most of the people in the neighborhood were Jewish; we were correct on that assumption. But they were, for the most part, retired and either on pensions or Social Security. They were not prone to make daily or even weekly bank transactions, and their accounts could in no way be called active.

The Rockaway branch was a disaster. But I don't want to leave the reader with the impression that every opening is a flop. Despite our famed sinking branch in Brooklyn, we made another stab at the borough a couple of years ago and bought into a thriving shopping center which had been established for some time and not only proved that it was doing good business, but also that it wasn't falling into the ground. The branch we opened was identical in square footage to the building which we had opened in the New Dodger Shopping Center, and we grievously underestimated how popular it would be. Despite our crowd pictures and our projections, the bank was too small from the day it opened.

Mobs — hundreds, thousands — flocked to the opening. We ran out of electric clocks, electric blankets, flatware. The police had to come and control the lines trying to fight their way into the bank. Customers tried in their own little way to swindle us by opening five or six $50 accounts and trying to collect five or six of the little $2.50 premiums, when they were limited to two gifts despite the number of accounts they opened. "But my nephew Marvin wanted an account," was the continual plea which rent the air that December evening in Brooklyn.

I suppose we should be delirious with a successful opening, but if we had done our calculations correctly we would have seen that the amount of square footage was going to be inadequate. I've visited the branch on a busy Friday afternoon and the operation is a mess: long lines at all of the windows, customers grumbling at the wait, tellers overworked and harassed, platform personnel snowed under. Obviously, we could do a lot more business if we had more space. But the original feeling was, what the hell, X amount of footage was okay for one part of Brooklyn, why shouldn't it be adequate for another part of Brooklyn? Extrapolate that a bit and you get, "All parts of Brooklyn look alike." It may look that way to the residents of Scarsdale, but people in Brooklyn know better.

We have, as I've said, 126 branches, and roughly 20 percent of those are losing money. Some are losing money because over the long haul the neighborhoods in which they had been profitable have run down. But most of the losers are new branches put up within the past five years. Losing money on bad judgment, not on bad conditions.

The lapses in logic that flowed out of Hiram's division were at times astonishing. We put up one branch in lower Manhattan simply so it could be near a branch of the New York City government, where we thought a lot of weekly and biweekly payroll checks would be cashed. Nice thinking, but merely running a check-cashing service will not support a bank.

Because banks are copycats, the same kind of mirror thinking which went into the development of our credit card carries over. We constantly compare our 126 branches to the two leaders in New York: Chase and First National City. If Chase has a total of 179 branches, with 8 branches on Staten Island, then our total of 126 branches would work out to 5.5 branches on Staten Island. What we don't know, of course, is whether Chase may be dying to close down four of their branches on Staten Island. But we do go ahead and build on Staten Island until we reach the 5.5 ratio or whatever the figure might be.

Not only are we anal retentive in our logic as to how many branches should be put up, we are equally foolish in selecting those whom we let do the putting up: we take an assistant manager originally from Michigan and put him in charge of planning for the Bronx. Forget that there are subtle changes in parts of the Bronx that politicians who have spent a lifetime there can't keep up with, much less an innocent from Michigan.

The staffing of a new branch always presents problems of disorientation. Because you simply cannot man a new bank with newly trained personnel, a process of cannibalization must take place. Knowledgeable tellers, platform assistants, loan representatives, assistant managers and the like have to be transferred from established branches and moved into the new branch. The personnel department, however, is infused with team and company spirit, and they consider it a singular honor when they inform a teller in the Bronx that he is among those chosen to move to the distant borough of Queens.

When it comes to lower ranking management personnel, the moves become much more difficult. Let's say that a man has laboriously risen from teller to chief teller to the platform, and finally he has been made an assistant branch manager. The chances are that he's an assistant manager in the same branch he's been working in all of his career (or at least in the same area). He has probably established a home in the area, he's familiar with the neighborhood businesses, and he is a proven asset to both us and the community. Suddenly, it's Queens. With no promotion.

The man has very little choice. If he turns down the transfer, we'll rank him only slightly above an employee caught with his hand in the till. He certainly doesn't want to uproot his family and start looking for new housing, worrying about new schools, and the like. So he probably faces the prospect of a two-hour combination subway and bus ride (each way) to his new job and the realization that the pressures on personnel in a new branch are infinitely stronger than in a well-established branch.

All personnel in a new branch have to put in exceptionally long hours until the branch gets on its feet, and the divisional and regional heads of the bank pay particular attention to it. As for the new manager and assistant manager, they have to go out and beat the bushes for business, and although they have earned their reputations already, if they fall down on the job with a new branch, the bank doesn't forget. Imagine, if you will, trying to make a new branch flourish when it is located next to a train station in Cedarhurst, Long Island.

All of New York City's banks are amalgams, the result of numerous mergers throughout the years. First National City, Chase Manhattan, Chemical, Bankers Trust, Manufacturers Hanover — all were formed by one bank merging with another. For number-hungry bank officials who want to show quantum jumps in deposits, earnings, number of branches, a merger is usually the easiest way. Yet even mergers can be extremely tricky, and I have to admit that First Mutual Trust, which is a crazy checkerboard of mergers made during the past hundred years, has not been too successful with our mergers.

Our most recent merger consisted of taking over a string of suburban New York banks, a small chain which numbered only ten branches in all but which covered a rich market where we always had wanted to be. We were blinded by the market potential and overpaid for the facilities. Although this bank was no more than one half hour from Manhattan, it was light years away in terms of banking.

Most of the branches were ramshackle buildings, more reminiscent of a one-room bank in a small midwestern town — the kind which is slowly dying after the new interstate highway was routed twenty miles away instead of through the town. Dusty, antique, staffed by awfully nice but incompetent personnel — this was the situation in the ten branches. That the banks were run fairly casually is an understatement. I happened to be in one of the branches one day when they ran out of money; the bank just didn't have enough on hand to cover withdrawals. The manager hurriedly put in a call to the branch in the next town, and in about twenty minutes a dusty station wagon pulled up with a tired-looking woman in her fifties at the wheel. She walked into the bank and said, "The money's in the trunk." One of the tellers stepped outside, opened the trunk, and there indeed were two sacks of loose money — about $10,000 worth.

There is a tendency for New York bankers to be condescending; in fact, we can be downright nasty about our colleagues outside of New York. But to see a teller casually walk to a station wagon and just as casually take out a couple of dirty sacks with loose money in them; well, that's more than I can handle. I said, "Aren't you worried about a robbery?" "Naw," came the reply, "and anyhow we know everyone in town, so they wouldn't dare rob us." The lady and her station wagon also served as the mail operation for the bank chain and twice a day she would make the rounds of the banks. One day, when another branch ran out of money and she had to make an emergency delivery of $15,000, her car got a flat. By the time she got the flat fixed the bank to which she was supposed to deliver the money was closed. So she did what came naturally in the sticks. She drove home and left the money sitting in the trunk of her car overnight. To her credit she called the bank which had closed on her and told them about the flat. And she also put her car in her garage — and locked the garage — that night.

When our chief of security, "Bullets" Loomis, took his first look at what passed for security in our latest acquisition, he practically fainted. Loomis, steeped in sophisticated electronic gadgetry, automatic cameras and instant replay, couldn't believe how things were run. Pasted throughout every bank in New York are pictures of bank robbers, past and present, with giant X's slashed through the photographs of those who have been nabbed. Whereas the walls of the banks in the suburban county were covered with photographs of winning basketball teams from the local schools. It took years of work and of hostility to get the new employees to take on our methods of security.

In one of our mergers in the distant past, we picked up a chain of banks located in and around New York City's garment center, a largely Jewish section of New York. Our people had no idea of what Yom Kippur was, and the first year that the Jewish high holy days rolled around, our banks, like the rest of the garment center, were absolutely deserted. Some of our personnel telephoned headquarters to find out if the plague had struck or if the city were under attack. In a merger of this sort, you automatically take on the officers of the old bank and generally you try to leave them in the positions they had held. Suddenly, our button-down officer corps found itself infiltrated with a large number of Als, and Harrys, all of whom seemed to wear off-green shirts and diamond pinky rings. The personnel department, not fond of pinky rings and feeling that colored shirts were not right for bankers, tried for a while to send some of our natural-shouldered specimens into the garment center. Our people were slaughtered. Suddenly we were granting loans to wig companies about to go under; we were heavily involved in financing cab drivers who wanted to go into the millinery business. The Als and Harrys were quickly sent back into the battle, and now that string of branches is extremely profitable.

The point in mergers is that each operation should be analyzed on its ability to become a profit center, not simply on its location in an area where you'd like to grow. In the case of the suburban chain, we could have done without ten ramshackle storefronts, which called themselves banks, and we should have built whatever we thought was necessary to cover the market. Our merger with the garment center bank, however, was an extremely good one, and after we got over our initial squeamishness about the kind of people the merger brought into the bank, the situation proved itself to be an excellent one.

Only occasionally do circumstances not relating to expansion lead to a merger. The most recent occurred in early 1973 when the New York State banking authorities tentatively approved a merger between the Jefferson Savings Bank in Watertown, New York, with the Community Savings Bank of Rochester. Although the New York State superintendent of banks had to invoke emergency provisions of the state's banking law to okay the merger, it seemed that federal approval also would be forthcoming.

It is unusual and almost impossible to secure approval for a merger between two banks which are situated in two different state banking districts. Essentially, such mergers are illegal: Bank A sticks to its turf, as does Bank B. But in the case of the Jefferson Savings Bank there seemed to be extraordinary circumstances which could only be solved by invoking emergency provisions in the state law. What went wrong? It's a little hard to tell, except in his first announcement about the merger the New York State superintendent of banking said that Jefferson Savings was a "problem" bank. Jefferson Savings is a bank known to have heavy commitments and high-risk loans in ghetto areas of New York City. The superintendent of banking, realizing that calling an institution a "problem bank" didn't endear it to its customers, later changed "problem" to "There exists . . . a substantial probability of future losses if these conditions are not promptly corrected."

What interested me was not the wrangling over the wordage, or even the fact that the United States controller of the currency, a gentleman named William B. Camp, stuck his two cents' worth in and said that in his view the proposal for merger was illegal. The fascinating aspect of what normally is a minor matter is that the touchy subject of race crept into the discussions. The implication was that a number of Jefferson's loans in ghetto areas had gone bad.

Banks in major cities handle the problem of race gingerly, and most of the time they reach the wrong decisions. About 20 percent of our branches are in full-fledged ghetto areas of the city, and although many of these branches are profitable, we would nevertheless like to close them down. This is never said in any official statement of the bank, but the implication is there all the time. None of these branches is new. Indeed, all of them are at least ten years old, and every one of them presents personnel problems that end up making them cost more than they are worth to the bank.

Staffing these branches is extremely difficult. No bank in New York is able to send white personnel into a branch in Bedford-Stuyvesant, and when we try to send blacks to the branch we run into resistance, too. One of our rising black officers was asked — actually, we begged him — to run a large branch in a ghetto area and he flatly said no. If pressed, he said, he would have to leave the bank, and he was too good an officer to lose. He said, "I wouldn't go into that neighborhood to work. These people will only mug the whites, but me they'll kill because I'm a symbol of success — I've given in to the white man's world."

What happens in these branches isn't hard to figure out. In any neighborhood disturbance, from a small street-corner fracas to a full-fledged riot, the bank — any bank — is usually a prime target. And it doesn't matter whether you've got red, white or blue personnel in the bank: your people are just as vulnerable. What we've started doing is simply boarding up the windows of our bank and battening down the hatches at the first sign of trouble. During holidays such as Martin Luther King Day, we have only a skeleton staff on duty and we're geared for trouble. And naturally, we are responsible for getting the staff to public transportation because of the hazards of walking to and from subways and bus stops.

The thrust of our thinking recently has been to strip many of our ghetto banks of staff and responsibility. We're not doing this by any particular design; because of the robbery rate of ghetto banks it is a necessity. Thus we will have a larger bank surrounded by several minibanks in a particular region. We can't shut down the branches; that requires too much red tape. But we can, and do, minimize the service we can offer. In the larger branch in the ghetto, all of our services are available. In certain sections of Queens, Brooklyn, and the Bronx, we've gone one step further. In response to complaints from large customers, we've opened what amount to cash depositories. No banking whatsoever goes on at these depots. Those businesses whose owners are afraid to go through the streets to make deposits at their regular branch are encouraged to go to one of the cash centers, which usually are situated in a fringe — i.e., safe — area of the ghetto. They simply drop off their money.

We're not alone, and if I know my bank, I'd say we're probably way behind in what can only be called "racial banking." Obviously, it's not what we should be doing, nor is it what any bank should be doing. We should be releasing capital at favorable interest rates to the ghettos. We should be encouraging home renovation, apartment and housing project construction. We should become engaged with our citizens and our neighborhoods; not disengaged. Yet bankers remain disengaged.

Ah, my critics will say, easy solutions to difficult problems. Well, I realize that they sound glib. But we should be doing more than my friend Hiram and his cronies are doing in branch location. He caught me in the hall the other day to complain about his latest problem. We've bought a lease on a location in Westchester County and we're about to install the latest branch of First Mutual Trust Company. The problem, Hiram says, is that the building we're going to be occupying used to be a Chinese restaurant, which went bankrupt. "I just don't know what we're going to do with the godawful smell of egg roll," Hiram says.

# CHAPTER VIII

AFTER the credit card debacle, my friend Oswald lay low for a good year and a half. He had a terrific career in the works, but down deep in his banker's heart he knew that he had come very close to blowing the entire thing with the Easy Buck Card. Although he had been angling for a marketing job, he finally felt that he was a little too hot to try for it so soon after the credit card mess. So he spent a year or so just fooling around. He drifted through national banking for a while, he scouted the trust department, he made friends with the international banking sharpies and soon affected an English accent and talked knowingly of "the drachma going to hell." But all of this was simply biding his time: he was after marketing.

The smartest thing he did was to become friendly with Lee Nevler, one of our most popular officers. Nevler literally doesn't do anything for First Mutual Trust Company except play golf: he's the best golfer in the bank. I know that this sounds strange, but if you recall, I mentioned that the national sport of banking is golf. The entire officer corps of First Mutual plays golf — and most of them are lousy golfers. Nevler had been an extremely good athlete when he was attending the University of Florida at Gainesville. In fact, he was captain of the golf team, and when he decided to come to New York and try his hand at big-time banking, little did he know how valuable his golf would become. As for his brain, well, it was composed primarily of grits with a few chitterlings thrown in. He was not one of your brighter types but he could hit a golf ball a mile.

Nevler's talent was first discovered when his immediate superior in equipment control (how many water carafes we have, how many typewriters and so forth) suggested they play golf one fine April day. Nevler showed up and casually shot a one over par on an extremely difficult Westchester County course. His boss was staggered, and Nevler modestly admitted that he was a pretty fair country golfer — scratch, actually — but he just didn't have the ambition to make it on the pro tour. Nevler even pointed out to his boss, a poor golfer named Jim, that the reason Jim was shanking was a loose left elbow. Thus was Nevler started as the house pro.

Nevler played golf with everyone in the bank. He filled out foursomes, he played with the president and the chairman; he was kept busy from the beginning of April until the end of October. Things were a little quiet during the winter, but that didn't bother Nevler much: he was an expert at wasting time. His promotions came through like clockwork; his salary rose comfortably.

Now Oswald had previously thought that the way to get ahead in a bank was to work like a dog, profess belief in the system, practice office celibacy, and pray for inflation — the friend of all bankers and the enemy of little old widows with shaky mortgages. Nobody told Oswald that to get ahead he had to know golf. But he soon discovered that in the upper levels of the bank there was more talk about golf than banking, sex, Nixon, peace, and the Federal Reserve. So he took up golf and went straight to Nevler with a flat-out proposition: for good old U.S. currency, he would pay for in-house lessons. Pretty soon Oswald and Nevler were a constant duo, playing hooky at every odd moment. In a year's time Oswald was shooting a respectable 12 handicap; a score not low enough to embarrass his superiors but good enough to make him a sought-after partner. He bided his time; then one fine Friday afternoon during June he wangled a game with the president himself and someplace between the fourteenth and fifteenth holes nailed down the appointment as the vice president in charge of marketing. The next day he packed his bag and hit the road, checking with his friends in banks throughout the country on how they put together their marketing plans. If you will recall, Oswald did some disastrous ripping off during his credit card days, but this time he was more careful. He decided that he couldn't trust anything that was given to him verbally; on this trip he brought back only that which he could find written documentation for and which seemed to be working.

Oswald also decided that, considering his previous experience with California banks, he could avoid potential pitfalls by staying away from the breezy ways of his fun-loving colleagues in the Far West. No, it was the good old stolid Middle West for Oswald, where men are men and there's no nonsense about sentimental mortgages or not foreclosing for emotional reasons; where the prime rate is a matter of reverence and genuflection. (Once, during an annual meeting of the entire officer corps of our bank, someone asked the chairman why the prime rate kept jumping around with little rational motivation. The chairman said, "Damned if I know. The only thing I know about the prime rate is what I read in the *Wall Street Journal*." We all laughed dutifully, because, of course, the chairman was funning. Or was he?) In the course of subsequent moves by our bank during the glorious days of 1970 and 1971 when the prime rate bounced around weekly, we traditionally looked like fools and many officers came to believe that the chairman got his information about the prime rate from *Screw Magazine*.

One of the cities Oswald hit during his swing through the American heartland was Cleveland, and he came back with an old marketing plan of one of the large banks. It is a remarkable document for dozens of reasons, not the least of which is that several of our marketing plans in the next few years showed an astonishing similarity to the Cleveland marketing plan. The most consistent characteristic of all marketing plans is that they seem to be written by marketing people who have little knowledge of what banking is today. There is a condescension which is hard to stomach. Listen to the motivation from the fellow who wrote the marketing plan: *The first monetary remuneration is that they [employees] get to keep their job. The second one is that if they do the job they are remunerated over and above what other people receive in the way of a salary.*

I like the implied threat most of all in that little remark; it's no-nonsense and very cut and dried. "We've been through merchandise award programs, cash award programs, vacation programs and what have you," wrote the banker from Cleveland, "and we found that it has a very definite bell curve effect to it. When this program is over, your sales efforts are over. So what we've attempted to do is to establish a program whereby [the branch manager] is entitled to invite so many of his people under an invitation over his signature to an annual sales dinner. They get to become members of the key club. They get, if they're a man, cuff links; if they're a woman, charm bracelets with the bank emblem. Gradually the key club is beginning to mean something more than bunnies [a reference to the Playboy key clubs] at the bank."

Well, what can one say about that? First, that if the hard-working employees in Cleveland are satisfied with cuff links, charm bracelets, and an annual chicken dinner, then Cleveland is really the sticks. But more, it is the attitude of the managerial mind which perpetrates such guff. If you were to put your employees on a percentage override, whereby they got a small percentage of business they brought in over a certain figure, then you'd see some action.

The pay scale of nonmanagement personnel is higher in New York than in Cleveland, as is the pay scale of junior officers who run branches. I don't know personally what the caliber of personnel is in Cleveland, but I'd bet that it is no better, and probably much worse, than our personnel. And our personnel stink. But this Cleveland tiger has no conception of what goes on in a branch, has no feeling for the people who work in it: *All we really expect of our tellers is that they know our services and know the benefits that these services have for our customers. We expect them to make friendly sales contacts. We expect them to be alert for opportunities, and the only thing that we ask them to do in a direct sales effort is to ask for the business. We don't care if they do nothing else than just ask for the business. We're firmly convinced that if we get our tellers to do nothing else but this we would increase our business tremendously. Finally, we do expect them to make salesworthy referrals to management.*

I will give you that life in Cleveland is not like life in New York: the folks in Cleveland live at a more leisurely pace. But I have been to banks throughout the country, and unless we are talking about Horseshoe, Wyoming, the pace in a metropolitan bank is fairly hectic. To expect $95 or $105 or even seasoned $125-a-week tellers to conduct a structured sales campaign as they try to cope with payday traffic is nonsense. In New York City I suspect that if a teller tried to take time to explain to a customer about our new "all-in-one statement" (whereby checking, loan, and savings balances are carried on one statement), the man standing in line behind the customer would have a few choice things to say. And if the teller went on to ask, "Would you like to enroll in the holiday club of your choice?" I know what would happen. (We, like all New York banks, are hilariously nonsectarian. We've got Christmas Clubs, Chanukah Clubs, and if the Seventh-Day Adventists or the Chinese pressed us, we'd honor their holidays, too. Give us your bread, baby, and we'll celebrate the Year of the Goat if you want us to.) Any red-blooded New Yorker when asked to enroll in a holiday club in the middle of February will tell the poor teller to get lost. Yet, here is this go-getter out in Cleveland spurring his troops on. If I sound cynical about it, I am, because I judge this kind of Mickey Mouse effort both as a customer and a banker.

*Finally, in the area of civic and public relations, the image that each one of these little branch offices has within its own community may be far different from the image that the Bank of Cleveland in total has, and it should be. The branch manager has the responsibility to see to it that the information is distributed. It may be distributed through his public-relations department, but it's his responsibility to see to it that it does get into the proper cir-cles.*

Image means nothing when just about every urban area in this country has either been ravaged by riots or is about to be burned down. *Branch managers are expected to know more about the makeup of that [their] area than anyone else in the bank.* Well and good, and also well and good that the branch manager is expected to know everything about that portion of the 1,156,000 households in his area, which contain a population with a median age of thirty years with a median income of $6,800 a year, living in homes with a median value of $13,000, and an owner occupancy of 67 percent. More than likely, the branch manager is simply trying to keep his head above water without staffing problems, pregnant tellers, clerks with acne, drunken guards, busted loans, bum mortgages. You can try and pay a man between $9,000 to $15,000 a year, as they might do in Cleveland, but that's all you get: $9,000 to $15,000 worth.

Banks around the country expect the branch personnel to go out into their neighborhood and cold canvass; i.e., to walk into neighborhood stores and shops without an introduction and try to drum up business. About all that ever gets done in New York is the hiring of a kid to stand outside the subway and give away flyers announcing the opening of a new branch in the neighborhood. Canvassing doesn't produce much in the way of new customers and small stores don't change their banks unless you can come up with a fantastic new policy. And if you do improvise a new system, the bank next door will have the same policy tomorrow.

As for knowing every pimple and every wart on every potential customer in your area, we try to tell our managers the same thing as well. But the population is changing so rapidly that the only stable areas these days are in Lake Forest or Palm Beach. In at least 20 percent of our branches, the managers aren't really thinking about going out and canvassing for new business; they're trying to get home safely without getting mugged or shot or both. Banks everywhere situated in marginal areas are simply hoping they won't be blown up or fire-bombed. I wish well the young and eager manager who decides to canvass the Bedford-Stuyvesant section of Brooklyn cold. Cold is what he will be.

Yet in Cleveland, where the world is turned over to metaphors, one of the bank's managers had this to say to the planners: *The population characteristics continue to show an increase of low-income families in the Euclid Avenue territory, with greater numbers of higher-income families moving to the suburbs. This trend has been bringing about a gradual decline in home value. The home values range from $8,000 to $20,000, with the majority of homes valued at $12,000.* The urban story in a nutshell. And nowhere in the report do the words "race problem" occur. Needless to say, the author of the report makes only an oblique comment to the violent changes that seem to be occurring in this neighborhood. He says the computer may well have some answers to the problem, and then follows with the thought that perhaps this bank's territory might be reapportioned. Gerrymandering is more like it.

Lest you think that there are enormous areas of difference in attitude between New York and the Middle West, console yourself with this sentence from Cleveland: *The film "How to Watch Pro Football" was shown at the local service club to which members of our management team belong. We have also arranged for three special showings, which in-*

*clude the local Boy Scout club and the dad's club at two of*
*the churches in the community.*

Sound a little — well, you might say just a little small
time? Not so. The jockstrap factor in banking, David Rockefeller and his suave bearing aside, plays an important role
with the ground-level troops. Every year one of our large
branches buys a block of tickets to one of the Army games
at West Point and transports a raft of enthusiasts up for a
day in the fresh air. It may well be the most important
piece of public relations done by that particular branch in a
given year. One year, when the red ink was running and the
budgets were shrinking, the main office suggested that it
seemed stupid to waste a lot of time and money on a trip to
a football game at West Point, at which the head of the
branch involved said pointedly that we would be endanger-
ing some $25 million in deposits if we were to cut out the
excursion. The mind cringes at the thought that serious
businessmen would even consider jeopardizing their relationship because of the loss of a game. However, it is astonishingly correct, and our officer heading that particular
branch was properly alarmed that his football game might
go by the board.

Our office which services the garment center on Seventh
Avenue has among its hidden assets several season tickets
to the professional basketball team, the New York Knicker-
bockers, which over the course of a season run about $450.
These tickets are discreetly given to our better customers on
a deliberate rotation basis, and they do us more good and
create more good will than all of the heady pronounce-
ments from our president or chairman.

At First Mutual Trust we are, like our colleagues in
Cleveland, constantly exhorting our managers, assistant

managers, and branch personnel to get out there and beat the bushes for deposits, checking accounts, loans, safe deposit box use, and on and on.

But if you think we, or any other bank, give our people lavish expense accounts or excess cash to do this beating of the bushes, you're wrong. We expect it to be done on the cheap, and nothing can beat a banker for cutting corners when he has to. One of our regions in the metropolitan area of New York City is composed of 25 branches, and one year the travel and entertainment budget of those 25 branches was $75,000, or roughly $3,000 a branch (I say roughly, because the $75,000 is not apportioned in equal amounts; larger branches will get more, smaller less, and so forth). Even taking a median figure of $3,000 per branch per year, this works out to about $60 a week. And this is entertainment and travel for perhaps four or five officers or management people who are specifically charged with increasing business. We have one office in Jackson Heights, Queens, which is just over the river from Manhattan, where the yearly budget is $900. For everyone. It works out to about $17 a week, or the price of a fair-to-middling meal for two people in Queens. And in case anyone in the Jackson Heights office has done a lot of traveling around in his car (at 10 cents a mile), he's liable to have chewed up the entire $17 that particular week.

A new branch of the bank was opened not long ago and their travel and entertainment budget was worked out to $1,800 for the first year. Here we've gone and sunk one hell of a lot of money in a new branch, put the damn building up, sent the troops out to fill this new branch with customers and money, and we've given them less than $40 a week to do it with. Still another of our branches in Queens (admittedly a small branch of the bank, but a functioning building nonetheless) was given an entertainment budget of $100 one year. When it was timidly pointed out by the man in charge of that branch that $100 (or $2 a week) barely covered the cost of visiting a customer, using public transportation, the bank relented and doubled the budget the next year (to $200) with the stern admonition that the branch had better start producing much more. If these figures strike you as a kind of parody, be my guest. They are an accurate reflection of the problems the man in the field has in dealing with the home office.

Another of our larger offices, with $35 million in deposits from commercial accounts, has a budget of $5,000 a year. No matter how you look at it, this branch is terribly valuable to us: $35 million turns over a lot of revenue for the bank. It strikes me — and others as well — that spending no more than $100 a week to protect (if you want to use that verb) $35 million is cutting your protection a bit thin.

First Mutual Trust Company's 126 branches range all the way from one-story holes-in-the-wall to elaborate two- and three-level modern branches. In each and every one of these branches we are vitally concerned about holding expenses down, increasing deposits — demand deposits and otherwise — because our branches represent our cash flow. True, we've an active international division, funding industries throughout the world, but they've got to have a source of cash for their investments. We are not primarily a trust company, with huge union and pension funds at our disposal generating gigantic revenues. And so we must depend on our retail operations for our cash needs.

In a typical medium to large branch we'll have a staff of fifteen people, but of those fifteen only one will be an officer. Generally speaking, we never assign more than one officer to a branch unless it is one of our largest.

The officer will either be an assistant treasurer or an assistant vice president, and he will likely have worked through the various training courses and will have a good credit background. There will be one general cage clerk and in addition another four tellers. Depending on the location of the bank, we usually will have a part-time teller who will come in on Fridays and Mondays to help with the heavier payroll and check cashing on those days. Normally, the part-time tellers are former full-time female tellers who got married and then decided to go back to work on a limited basis. There will be one vault clerk; he's the guy with the sleepy look on his face who resents your asking to use your safe deposit box. One guard with one nonfiring pistol, four or five platform assistants, a secretary, a typist or two, and there you have it.

In this particular bank, there might be demand deposits of $5 million, and in the category of demand deposits you've got checking accounts (regular and special) and savings accounts (with all of their beautiful permutations). Beyond the $5 million there probably will be another $3 million in fixed-time deposits, home mortgages, installment loans, and advance checking loans. All in all, a tidy little business with $8 million to be accounted for. The expenses of running the branch might run to $450,000. This breaks down to rent, salaries, overhead, travel and entertainment, depreciation, unresolved differences, overtime, agency help, plus the charges from our operations division. The branch is charged for check processing, installment lending, marketing, business development, administration, and branch training. The auditing division throws its two cents in, as does public relations, telephone, medical. Generally, we calculate that the $5 million will produce income of $500,000, which is 10 percent on our money, but then, we allow the branches a 9 percent profit on any excess of funds, which produces a little more income. (Excess of funds simply means the amount of money in the bank above and beyond that money allocated for expenses.) Actually, the total income from this bank is about $725,000, and after all of the charges are taken out, the net profit is roughly $136,000. Remember, we're dealing with a bank which has $8 million lying around, and the net income is a little less than 2 percent of the total deposits.

No matter how you slice it, it's not that much profit. Multiply $136,000 by our 126 branches, and you wind up with about $17 million in net profit from the retail side alone. Now that's a better figure, but it still isn't enough. Most banks, if you search hard enough through the annual reports, are owned by one family, or the controlling interest is held by one family. The Rockefellers and Chase Manhattan are the outstanding example of one-family ownership. Thus, while banks are public companies, and their shares are traded in major markets, the influence, behind the scenes, is oftentimes familial.

Our bank, for example, is controlled by an irascible old man in his eighties whose nephew is our chairman. Blood tends to be thicker than currency when it comes to banks. (I will digress momentarily to point out that family-owned banks can sometimes find themselves in embarrassing situations. In one of the most prominent banks in New York, the chairman was even more prominent than the bank, and his brother was equally prominent in the city. But the brother had a son who was regarded as the black sheep of the family. The son had his trust fund at the family bank, as did all of the members of that particular family. What no one knew was that one year the black sheep turned over the proceeds of his trust fund to the Weathermen, a charitable donation which raised the hackles of the entire family. And the FBI as well, who came charging into the bank one day to find out what the Weathermen were doing with a check from the bank. After a bit of hemming and hawing and vague references to the younger generation the affair was settled, but not without giving the chairman, his brother, and assorted aunts and uncles pause.)

Getting back to our irascible owner, his problem is simple. If our stock earned $4.80 last year, that's got to be improved this year, come hell or higher inflation. Uncle tells Nephew "Get the earnings up," and the word permeates the bank slowly and uncertainly.

Every year, in every bank in the world, the phrase "submit your plan" is heard throughout the banking land. The creaky procedure begins in the fall of the year before the budget is applicable. In the fall of 1973, the banking world is fumbling about what the economic state of their bank will be in 1974. Forecasting is an uncertain business at best. When the government decides it has a yen for the yen and the dollar is worth less than it was last year, then budget and planning is made even more difficult. On top of all of this is our Uncle, Marc by name, who tells his nephew Alan to get the goddam earnings up, the stock is losing favor with the security analysts.

The tendency of every division of the bank when it

comes to making a plan is to play it safe and use the banker's rule of thumb: to wit, when in doubt pray that everything will go up 10 percent. The 10 percent dictum is universal; my friend Oswald found that in Cleveland when they talked knowingly of increasing business next year, they always talked in increments of 10 percent. Or if it looks like you can't make the 10 percent, then bail out of the business entirely. As one of our planners wrote: *We are practically out of the business of construction loans. Demand continues to be strong. We anticipate that we will be confronted with the necessity of turning down large numbers of loan requests and for this reason we project no fee income for construction loans after the first quarter.*

It's simple to see what happened here: we made far too many construction loans three, four, and five years ago when interest rates were young and gay and a good couple of points lower than they are now. You can't renege on the loans, as each year the builders show up on your doorstep and ask for their portion due under the original terms. We made a loan at a lower rate and, by golly, our ace economist, Dr. Peter Mayer, our vice president and prolific market-letter writer, failed to guess that inflation was going to strike and that interest rates were going to soar. Despite Dr. Mayer, one of our officers wrote: *In view of the excessively high cost of money, some projects have become uneconomical. Also, changes being proposed in the tax laws which reduce the amount of tax shelter available are discouraging further activity. Our present goal of keeping our construction loan portfolio at an average figure of _____ will be continued. But this will be difficult to accomplish unless we are successful in laying off a significant portion of these loans.*

"Laying off" is another way of saying we discovered a method of getting rid of some of the peskier construction loans by factoring them. *In view of our recent affiliation with James & Silberman, we propose to talk with them about the possibility of placing some of our portfolio with their clients. We have set a goal of _____ million of our presently outstanding loans.* In other words, head for the hills. New York City may be a blight, but don't look to us for any help during reconstruction. The numbers don't look good.

In putting a statement like this into the annual budget, the head of the construction loan division is not only playing it safe, he is being devastatingly honest with the top management so he doesn't have to explain himself six months from now.

As for home mortgages, we wouldn't go out of our way to give a mortage to the chairman's mother. *We are continuing to meet the requests of our customers for home mortgages. We don't have to solicit them; our customers come to us. The volume, however, has dropped substantially from a year ago, which we ascribe to the exceedingly high prices at which properties are being sold with the one-third down payment in cash required. And because of the tight money situation and the increased cost of construction, the number of housing starts has declined and further declines are anticipated until the money situation eases.* Translation: Go to a savings and loan institution for a mortgage, don't come to us. Further translation: If we could find a decent way to lay off our existing home mortgages, the way we've done with construction loans, we'd be just as happy. But it's a little trickier because if a customer who had been paying his mortgage to First Mutual Trust Company suddenly wakes up one day and finds that his mortgage is held by the Kaminsky Second Mortgage and Storm Door Company, why the customer might get a bit nervous. And take his money out of his checking account.

Another headache enjoyed by the home mortgage troops was pressure placed on the bank by its large customers: *"We have had pressure from some of our large accounts in the National Department to make loans with their employees who are moving into this area or from city to city in our service area. We have done so for a number of people at American Can when they moved to Connecticut several years ago. We have also received inquiries from IBM, Squibb, and International Nickel, and we have to make some policy of how to respond to such inquiries to prevent the volume of loan requests from getting out of hand."* That treacherous little phrase "make some policy" is your average, influence-prone bank at work in the good old American tradition. No, don't come walking off the streets to us for a loan, but if you happen to be working for one of our customers in another division, why maybe we can work something out.

Oswald picked up the lingo of planning quite rapidly, and though I don't think he would have the nerve to reproduce verbatim the marketing boys' report from Cleveland, the spirit was the same. Which means that almost all of the budget and planning people have heads beveled from the same piece of knotty pine. *"The primary objective of the Queens-Nassau area is to maximize profit through mounting and sustaining a big demand on depositing effort on both the commercial and retail levels and by increasing the profit of existing relationships. The second part of the effort is to be realistic about balance compensations, charges for services, the elimination where possible of free services, and the development of all possible affiliated business."* The street translation is, no free checking privileges for any customer unless the balance kept by the customer is so staggeringly large (and thus, correspondingly foolish on the part of the customer) that we have to give him free service. *"We want to be certain particularly that every platform person is delegated specific responsibility in a given area and understands what is expected of him and that he is given guidance and training where required provided the information needed to perform effectively measures with the progress."*

When I said before that the planning begins in the fall, I was overstating it by a bit. Actually, planning reports are distributed to everyone in a managerial capacity on July 1 and are due to the comptroller on September 30. Summaries are sent back to division and regional heads, and then forwarded to the first vice presidents in charge of national, international, retail, and trust. The first vice presidents either accept or reject the summaries, saying, Yes, your earnings goal is right on the button, or no, your earnings just aren't high enough. The negotiation continues throughout the fall, and as Christmas approaches the president and the chairman get increasingly restive until all of the numbers are in. Goals are adjusted up, down, sideways — you name it, we shove it around.

The whole package finally reaches the executive committee deep into the fall and they take a long look at the totals. Since the idea of all American business is growth, the executive committee has an *idée fixe* as to what those numbers should show *regardless of whether they actually reflect the real world or not.* The totals might show the bank how to increase its earnings by perhaps 4 or 5 percent and these totals might be the careful distillation of literally thousands of hours of work. The chairman then nervously takes the final number to his uncle and invariably (or so the rumor is) gets yelled at. No matter how good the numbers are, Uncle Marc yells at nephew Alan, who grins and bears it. Let us say, hypothetically, that no matter how the numbers are fudged, our earnings must go from $4.50 a share to $4.70 a share. Uncle Marc's blood pressure goes up correspondingly. He simply tells his nephew to take those numbers and dispose of them and come back with a higher figure. Our chairman, the nephew, goes to the executive committee, clears his throat, looks at the next plane out for Palm Springs, and says, "Gentlemen, these figures just aren't good enough, especially the way the economy is booming. I wish you'd go back to the drawing board and see if you can't increase earnings by another .20 a share." And off he goes.

The executive committee says those magic words, "Adjust your goals," and the word spreads throughout the bank, "Increase the goals by 8 percent." For the next two weeks or so, we all start kidding ourselves, our superiors, and the world because we start to lie with the numbers, and as every gambler will tell you, the numbers don't lie. Not often, anyway. For every ten cents in increased earnings to our stock, we should do another million dollars in profits. To get that million, you have to produce $1,500,000 in gross income, less $500,000 in expenses, taxes, and so on. And up go the earnings. What happens when we casually dump three or four million in one fiscal year to a credit card? Down go the earnings, .30, .40, or .50 a share.

The square management officers in the bank submit honest plans. The sharpies know that the top management always caves in and asks for a 10 percent increase, no matter what the conditions. The squares usually have to stay late and work and revise their numbers. Eventually everyone from Staten Island to Rome hits 10 percent. The sharpest of them all leave loopholes in their budget estimates to management. Consider Oswald's swan song: *In spite of the emphasis given to the planning program, the money market conditions during the past year and the apparent continued economic factor make the forecasting of demand deposits considerably more difficult this year; most of the mature branches have easily identified those deposits which might leave the banking system at any time.* Folks, since the market is going to hell in a basket, we don't really know if people are going to be stupid and leave their money in their nonproductive checking accounts. In addition, we've spotted those commercial accounts which just might be going to the wall. *Should interest rates go down, our projections should be easy to achieve and in fact would be achieved. However, should interest rates go higher or even stay the way they are, there will be a continued drain on these deposits. In either event the effort made to increase and retain demand deposits will be increased from what it has been.* He's covered himself for just about any emergency except a typhoon. If the rates go down, everyone will be in the chips, but in that aside he's reminding his superiors all up the line that the chance of interest rates dropping and *staying down* is practically nil. Even if they don't go up, he's covered himself with glory by stating things are going to be tough even if the rates stay the same. Giving Oswald his due, he wrote an honest report — cagey, but honest. His superiors rejected it and said, kindly increase demand deposits by

10 percent. There are some days when the stupidity overwhelms even the junior members of the club.

The most nervous dudes of all during budget and planning time are the officers in investment and trusts who live and die by what the crazy Dow Jones Industrial Average does. They can forecast until they're blue in the face, but if the market decides to go to hell even the professionals are caught, and that includes banks. They simply say, "Sure, we'll produce an increase of 10 percent in our portfolios and let it go at that."

Occasionally the tension during all of this planning wreaks a different kind of havoc. One fall, one of our branches opened an account for a "show-biz" chimp. When a senior vice president wanted to know what the hell we were doing with an account for a monkey, the response was that the branch made a precedent-shattering decision. Since the monkey could sign an X, they figured okay, open the account. But if the animal (or parrot) can't sign an X, let 'em go to Chase.

# CHAPTER IX

**E**VERYONE here remember the Penn Central? Well, there is neither time nor space to go into any of the fascinating details about how that esteemed organization went down the toilet. (There are more elegant ways to describe going into bankruptcy, but, as far as the Penn Central is concerned, I think the figure of speech is well deserved.) But aside from being a classic case of corporate skulduggery, numbskullery, bad management and out and out rape (the victims being those innocents who bought the stock as the railroad was about to plunge into bankruptcy), it is a perfectly valid example of how banks get in bed with American corporations, and vice versa.

Back in the spring of 1971 Chairman Wright Patman (Dem., Tex.), relying on a report prepared by a subcommittee of the House Banking and Currency Committee, charged Chase Manhattan with getting rid of 436,300 shares of worthless Penn Central stock about three weeks before the railroad went bankrupt. All of this stock-dumping took place in May 1970, and the railroad filed for reorganization under the bankruptcy laws the next month. Mind you, Chase bailed out at about 14, and when the announcement was made public the stock fell to 6. What interested the House Banking Committee was that Chase had been a pretty good friend of Penn Central, in fact, such a good friend that they had lent them $50 million in cash. (Lest one accuse Chase Manhattan of being a fair-weather friend, they weren't the only bank running for the hills in the debacle. Morgan Guaranty Trust sold 370,000 shares; Continental Illinois got rid of 326,000 shares, Security Pacific National Bank made 24,000 shares go away, United States Trust Company unloaded 18,000 shares. They also managed to bail out before the rest of the world learned how shaky the railroad was.)

The committee report said that it was Chase's loan department, sitting with $50 million in notes, which advised its own trust department that the railroad was about to go under, and for the sake of good old Chase get rid of the stock. The banking committee felt that Chase's loan department tipping off Chase's trust department was an unfair advantage over the millions of plain working stiffs who knew nothing about the Penn Central except that it didn't work too well. Chase vehemently denied the charges.

There is a contradiction in the banking committee's report. They point out that nine major financial institutions (of which six were banks) dumped 1.8 million shares of Penn Central prior to the bankruptcy announcement, and yet the committee specifically named Chase in its report. My feeling is that every financial institution had some kind of inside knowledge about Penn Central — thus the incredible dumping of stock.

But the banking committee's point in their report was that Chase the lender was informing Chase the shareholder to get out. Chase, in categorically denying these charges, said they had an absolute policy against any flow or incidental communication of inside information that one department might be receiving. Chase said its trust department made its decision on the first quarter results of 1970, which were terrible, plus a change in the attitude of a Philadelphia brokerage house that previously had strongly recommended the stock. When the brokerage house said sell, don't buy, Chase said what's good for a Philadelphia brokerage house is good for us. (The senior partner for the brokerage house just happened to have spent many happy years as a member of the Penn Central's board of directors.)

What's the truth here? My guess — and it simply is a guess — is that there's a bit of truth on both sides of the argument. One junior officer in the loan department of Chase would not be beyond picking up the telephone and calling his fellow junior officer in the trust department and saying, "Harvey, get rid of Penn Central, the bottom is going to fall out." Or the exchange of information could indeed have been on a much higher level; the head of one division taking two Gelusils at lunch and telling the head of the other division the disaster was about to strike. But any market analyst with half his marbles could have looked at the first quarter results of Penn Central, seen that they were hair-raising, and then, when the Philadelphia brokerage house came in with a sell recommendation, put two and two together without any trouble. My hunch is a combination of both. (And, of course, it is impossible to prove by any kind of interrogation — under oath or not — because bankers know how to lie pretty well.)

The reason I have exhumed the soiled laundry of the Penn Central is that it is a lovely example of very high-level influence at work. The name of the game in banks is influence, from the smallest branch right up to the top. Banks are usually quite defensive about the role they play; their critics, however, are not swayed by their innocence. The most persistent critic of banking in the United States today is Chairman Patman of the House Banking and Currency Committee. Patman has waged a long, lonely, and undoubtedly frustrating fight against the power of banks. In recent years Ralph Nader, always alert for new investigative opportunities, has looked longingly at the private preserve of Patman. And, in fact, in 1972 Nader's investigators took on First National City Bank of New York in a flurry of publicity. First National City beat Nader handily. His report was page one news for one day and then it (the report) and he (Nader) moved onward and upward; currently Nader is investigating the insurance industry. Patman, on the other hand, is no Johnny-come-lately to banking. He's made a lifelong crusade of it.

David Rockefeller claims that the reason Patman has said a plague on all of your banking houses is that he was turned down for a loan when he was a youth. Patman, who does his homework with care, rejects this simplistic explanation and continues to bombard the public with statistics about the enormous power of banks. In the February 17, 1973, issue of the *New Republic,* Patman listed the horrendous fact that commercial banks now control assets of over $900 billion, or just a few savings accounts away from a trillion dollars. "The concentration of economic resources of this magnitude would be serious enough by itself, but the problem is aggravated by the multiple functions and powers of commercial banks. Banks are quasi-monopolies. Their basic product, credit, is the lifeblood of commerce; their power to grant or withhold this commodity is a source of built-in intimidation that hangs over all areas of the economy." Patman says that in his committee's survey of the largest 49 banks in the United States located in ten major cities, he found more than 8,000 interlocking directorships between these banks and more than 6,500 companies. "More than 750 of these interlocks were with 286 of the 500 largest industrial companies in the United States. The same pattern of interlocking relationships was discovered between these 49 banks and each of the 50 largest merchandising, transportation, utility and life insurance companies. It is absurd to think that banks ignore the holdings of their trust departments when they face major loan decisions. It is equally absurd to think that a bank will ignore the needs of its holding company subsidiaries."

The example Patman cites in his article is the near-collapse of the Lockheed Aircraft Corporation, a chilling one, well documented and almost as well publicized as the Penn Central fiasco.

During much of 1971, the governments of Great Britain and the United States became extremely nervous about the fate of the Lockheed airbus. Hurried bailout efforts were launched for Rolls Royce, the producer of airbus engines in Great Britain, and for Lockheed, the builder of the airframe in the United States. Behind all the rescue efforts were some of the nation's largest commercial banks, whose lobbyists swarmed over Capitol Hill on behalf of the loan guarantees. The tracks of the banks — led by Bankers Trust and Bank of America — were found at every turn. First, the banks had $400 million out in lines of credit to Lockheed. Then it was discovered that many of the same banks also had lines of credit out to subcontractors. . . .

The Lockheed debacle, thank God, did not touch First Mutual Trust Company, but it could easily have. We, too, are littered with interlocking directorships, and Patman is not indulging in idle rhetoric when he says that the banks have unbelievable power in many parts of the economy.

To give you some idea of how interlocking directorships work, I can say that we have an interlocking directorship with a prominent aircraft manufacturer. Let's call them Spitfire Aircraft Manufacturing Company. Although their headquarters are in the Middle West, they have manufacturing facilities and plants in literally every section of the United States. One of our most senior officers sits on the board of Spitfire, attends board meetings, and so forth.

Of late, Spitfire has been having its troubles. Deeply tied into the aerospace industry, Spitfire has been trying to find sensible ways of widening its base. They don't want to be dependent solely upon our building new bombers or missiles or sending monkeys to Mars. Spitfire has found it just too damned risky depending on defense contracts. Well, why not? It certainly makes sense. Perhaps at one of the board meetings a Spitfire executive even told his First Mutual Trust boardmember that Spitfire was thinking of getting into other fields, like offshore oil speculation.

The sequence of events is a little complicated, but it began with a telling excerpt from a report from one of the research units of our bank:

Many recommendations have been made such as investment research and municipal bonds. *The group was recently able to be of assistance to Spitfire Aircraft* [my italics], which is considering the desirability of investments in offshore oil exploration. There has been a growing number of large national corporations wishing to get into the offshore oil business, and it is hoped that our research group can be helpful in this regard.

That, kiddies, is the old-school, terribly polite, awfully proper influence. I can recall other reports written by other divisions in the bank saying that offshore oil exploration stinks these days, and First Mutual Trust shouldn't be putting a cent into it. But this independent, free-thinking group says they've been fortunate in being of assistance to the folks at Spitfire. Is Spitfire planning to drill a few offshore oil wells in Long Island Sound? I don't know, nor does the report say. But we've been of help.

Now there is absolutely nothing in the record which would link Spitfire with First Mutual Trust except that interlocking directorship. Surely nothing can be proved, short of bugging our officer's navel prior to his sitting in on Spitfire board meetings. And even then we would show more taste. Gently said, gently heard by our officer. Who knows what our officer did after that? Maybe he flew back to New York and kept his mouth shut. Maybe he had a word with our chairman; perhaps he mentioned Spitfire's need to the research unit. All I know for sure is that Spitfire popped up out of left field in the research unit's report; it was, in fact, the only company mentioned by name. And further, one of our officers sits on Spitfire's board. A tenuous connection? Yes, it's tenuous, but it doesn't take a raving paranoid to watch our dealings with Spitfire with interest. And, I hasten to point out, there is nothing illegal here. Not one bit. Except — and it is an awfully large exception — one can only wonder if another company having oil fever would receive the same treatment as Spitfire is going to. This is banking influence, albeit done with a lot of class. If, of course, Spitfire were in the same shape as Lockheed in 1971, well, then you haul out the lobbyists and you forget about niceties. Spitfire's case is much more typical than Lockheed, and not comparable at all to the dumping of the Penn Central stock.

Can you outlaw this sort of thing? Of course not. It isn't illegal, it doesn't violate any statute that I can think of, but it does point out what Patman has been saying about interlocking directorships and all they can mean to a bank and its customers.

A neat little game is played on the upper levels of directorsmanship: you put your man on our board and we'll put our man on your board. Any cursory examination of any bank's board of directors immediately reveals a raft of outsiders from America's largest corporations: electronics, oil, aircraft, automobiles, cigarettes, food, conglomerates — every industrial area of the country is represented.

Our board of directors comprises an illustrious group of men whose names are instantly recognizable not only to readers of the business pages of newspapers, but to the general reader as well. Not very surprisingly; for every company represented on our board, we've been fortunate to land our officers on the board of every one of those companies. And that is interlocking directorships. Do the outside members of the board exert any pressure on our trust policies, our lending policies? I have no idea, but I would suspect that any dealings are done as quietly as was our assistance to Spitfore Aircraft.

Congressman Patman does not discuss directorships on the lower level; he's only concerned with the top political and management structure of banks and corporations. Yet a fascinating interweave of directorships takes place in all banks on a middle management level, completely hidden from the eyes of the public as well as from the Patmans of the world. It's all done through channels, all done correctly, but the relationships exist.

A Bronx savings and loan institution wanted one of our

officers to join their board of directors. Our officer, Michael Fine, wrote the following letter:

A friend of mine, Kevin Nathan, who is a director of Bronx ————, has put my name forth as a possible director of this savings and loan association. I told him that I would be pleased to serve if selected but I would have to receive approval from First Mutual Trust Company. The proposal is still at the talking stage. But, as things now stand, I will get in touch with Chairman James Prashker when we have made our decision.

Fine then attached the most current statement of the savings and loan association, listing assets, cash and government bonds, first mortgage loans, and reserve and surplus. Also attached was a complete list of the board of directors. Under Chairman Prashker's name Fine wrote: "Mr. Prashker is very prominent in Catholic affairs in the Bronx, and he even has been knighted by the pope."

First Mutual then did a little checking, and another memo found its way into the files:

In connection with Mr. Fine going on the board, we checked with Millard Marmur about the fact that Mr. Prashker has been knighted by the pope and is active in Catholic affairs in the Bronx. Mr. Marmur said that this would have no effect on Mr. Fine's relationship with the diocese, since the deposits are arranged by the bishop and not known to the laity. Another thing is that we now have about all the deposits from the Bronx we can get.

If any of you reading this have been knighted by the pope, then you know what a terrible inner struggle all of this must have been to all parties concerned. Of all the sentences in this exchange, the one which knocks me out is the line to the effect that we've milked the Catholic coffers dry in the Bronx, so don't worry about anybody accusing us of a conflict of interest.

Why would a Bronx savings and loan institution want one of our officers on their board? I can think of two dozen reasons. Here's one of the reasons from the memo:

Mr. Marmur said that he would have trouble finding reasons to turn down Michael Fine's request to serve as a director. Mr. Marmur also feels that no undue problems would crop up. Mr. Marmur says that many savings associations like to have a commercial banker on their board.

Done and done; welcome to the Bronx, Mr. Fine, and if our chairman takes a shine to you, maybe we can get you knighted by the pope, too.

Nothing illegal here. And awfully careful was First Mutual Trust. Yet one criticism of such arrangements, among many, is that once the deed is done — i.e., the directorship allowed — there seldom if ever is a followup. I realize that, with the pope plus acres of bishops watching over this particular savings and loan institution, nothing could ever go awry. But things sometimes go awry, banks do go downhill, ownerships do change, sometimes the M*f*a does get its hands on banks, and then presto, we have an officer on the board of an institution which might be used to funnel skimmed money from Las Vegas casinos. It probably won't happen, but it's that one in a million shot which can ruin banks. Or what if a flock of mortgages suddenly go bad in the Bronx, and the savings and loan institution needs some ready cash fast? Would we give them undue advantage if they came to us to be bailed out? Michael Fine, wisely, would not be involved in any way if the savings outfit needed money. But he could make his presence felt, and we would be well aware that he sat on their board. My feeling is that Patman is correct about directorships on the highest level, but that he should also be concerned about them on the lowest level as well.

Don't think for a moment that First Mutual Trust, like any other bank, isn't aware of all of the pitfalls. The subject has come up from time to time; what we usually do, whenever morality rears its ugly head, is quick, run a check to see what other banks in New York have for a policy. What we find, every time, is that banks officially do not like their officers sitting on the boards of small- or medium-sized companies; they want all such requests to be approved on the highest level; and they tend to discourage any participation. (Invariably those banks with the most rigid strictures against their officers sitting on other boards are those banks with the most dubious interlocking relationships on the very highest levels.)

During one such soul-searching period at First Mutual, the following memo was produced. It gave arguments against and for our officers sitting on other boards. Interestingly, in the "against" section, a rebuttal was handily provided for anyone who might be at all confused as to where the real issues lay.

2. Directorships might be influential in the floating of new stock issues or in other financial transactions because of implied bank approval or sponsorship. (This can be avoided by carefully looking into motives, management, and future transactions.)

3. The loss of business impartiality as a lending officer. (Not different from other relationships that usually develop between a bank's officers and its customers.)

4. A waste of officer's time. (Need be no greater than in any customer relationship and can be kept to a minimum.)

5. Possibility of being regarded as a watchdog arrangement by the bank. (Not interpreted in today's business thinking.)

6. The chance that financial gain may occur to the bank because of its officer's actions as a board member. (This is a remote possibility in board membership but one that doesn't cause undue embarrassment.)

And those were the negative sides of the question, neatly rebutted at every turn. On the plus side, the floodgates opened:

1. An officer-directorship gives the bank ranking position as a provider of banking services for the company. [Here, rather than a counterargument, the "rebuttal" is simply supporting.] (This is particularly valuable when a growing company goes public.)

2. As protection against competitors. (Some of our competitors are pushing officers to serve on customers' boards.)

3. Board membership gives a bank officer a closer chair to company and industry progress.

Thus, the positive side. You'll note that the author of the memo obviously wanted as much participation in other companies' boards as possible. In our finite wisdom, however, we still are diffident about our officers joining smaller companies. Larger, New York Stock Exchange–listed corporations are swell for our president and chairman.

At times, the pressure of the amount of money that a customer has with us is just overwhelming, and not only would we allow our officers to sit on their board, we'd send the chairman over every Thursday to do the Venetian blinds if the customer wanted it:

"Michael Seligman [of the Seligman Company retail store chain] has lunch with the writer [an officer seeking permission to join Seligman's board]." The officer quickly points out that the Seligman Company maintains average monthly balances with us which exceed $2.8 million. This is a lot of change, and in case nobody was listening, the officer quickly adds that Michael Seligman has all kinds of accounts with us including his personal account of over $5 million, and several trust accounts. Then, the officer adds that the company recently went public, and on top of all the other money of the Seligman crew we were handling, the proceeds of the issue also are flowing through our eager hands. "Mike says that the New York Stock Exchange has asked his company to add one member to his board. Mike points out that when they went public he asked that I come on the board, but I could not accept then. He hopes now that I can join. There is sufficient personnel at our Madison Avenue branch and at loan administration division to handle the company without my participation. Seligman Company has a young management team and has been growing for the past number of years."

The officer who put together this request and shipped it through channels was very shrewd; he knew that the sight of all those Seligman millions possibly falling into the wily hands of a competitor would provoke a response. His request was sent all the way up to the top, was approved with vigor, and came back down in seven days — a record. The endorsements tell part of the story: "I am told they are high-grade people whose business is actively solicited by other banks. Strongly recommend approval."

I like especially the "high-grade," as differentiated from the regular animals in the retail clothing business. We have no more idea if they're high grade or about to go under than the man in the moon. But we do know how to read how many millions they've locked up with us, and if they picked their noses in public they'd still be high grade.

Essentially, our policy is to say no, and yet the files are full of stories of exceptions. Essentially, our policy should be to say no and make no exceptions. And essentially, America is not built that way. "Let me introduce you to my friend John," is the way we conduct our business, and banks aren't an exception.

If the SEC is so tough on violators of the insiders' trading laws, then banks surely should be as stringent. The problem, as always, is enforcement. Banks are privy to an enormous amount of information about the companies they do business with. Any officer can scan the monthly cash flow and tell if a Penn Central is in the making. Put a bank officer on the board of directors and the access to information trebles. Do bank officers openly violate any laws concerning insiders' information? Not in our bank, and I doubt in any other large bank either. But then again we're not checking the stock-trading accounts of a stray nephew who just happens to have an uncle who works at the bank and has managed to divine that Penn Central is going to hit the rocks in a few days. How does the Pentagon control those officers who have insiders' information prior to the letting of a huge government contract? Well, they can't control a man's bank account. Nor can we control our officers. Yes indeed, we spell it out quite clearly in all of our Officers Handbooks. Where all bankers thread the needle is in our desire to help our bank. We sure don't want the Seligman family and their millions to leave our balance sheet. Banks live and die by their compensating balances; that is, the amount of money an account lets lie fallow, thus putting it at our disposal to earn income for us. If ethics are stretched, they usually are bent for the bank's welfare and not for that of an individual.

If an officer wants to fool around, he does it like Herman Arthur Bonhag, who is fifty-three years old and was a trusted employee of First National City for thirty-five years. He went to work for the bank at the age of eighteen, and after thirty-five years had worked his way up to an assistant vice presidency and the managership of a branch. In January of 1961 something evidently slipped in Herman's noggin, because for the next five years he managed to loot several accounts under his stewardship of more than $1 million. He didn't fool around with any inside information: he simply (according to a federal grand jury) transferred the money to fictitious accounts he'd set up.

Banks live in perpetual terror of the Herman Arthur Bonhags of this world. That they only pay people like Bonhag $15,000 or $20,000 a year doesn't seem to sink in to the top management. Only when someone like him gets away with a million or so do they wake up to the idiocy of underpaying those officers directly responsible for the money in the vault.

But this is a pretty far cry from officers and the influence they can and do exert. The directorship problem is one that crops up frequently at all banks. I haven't touched on the headache of stock tips, insiders' information, and those very gray areas concerning the stock market. There is nothing we can do, short of bringing in the FBI, to keep tabs on whether our officers use information they have access to to make personal gains in the stock market. We do have very stringent rules; enforcement is mostly a matter of trust.

Influence is exerted by banks in Washington and in state legislatures throughout the country. In 1973, members of the Senate Banking Committee debated behind closed doors whether to open their committee meetings to the public when they debated various issues before their committee. The ubiquitous Jack Anderson reported on the debate in his syndicated column. Anderson said that senators on the banking committee like John Tower, a Texas Republican, and John Sparkman, an Alabama Democrat, received "enormous financial support" from "the nation's bankers" and led the fight to keep all hearings of the Senate Banking Committee in executive session. Anderson claimed that those senators who fight for the rights of the banking industry like to do their fighting screened from public view. Anderson quoted Sparkman in the meeting as saying, "I foresee disturbances. . . . I just can't conceive of successful sessions of marking up bills with the doors open."

Those on the committee leading the fight for more public access to information were Senator William Proxmire (Dem., Wisc.), who said that all of the committee's hearings should be public except those which deal with classified data and legitimate business secrets.

The issue was closed quickly and firmly by Tower, who said that before the Senate Banking Committee did anything they ought to take the entire matter to the floor of the Senate. Anderson said Tower's move to bring the question to the Senate amounted to killing the issue, because the Senate itself was for more, rather than less, secrecy in its dealings.

I wouldn't say that we lobby in Washington with the same zest that the gun lobby operates; after all, bankers are supposed to be a bit more dignified than gun-toting members of the National Rifle Association. But we do our best; we do more than get our two cents' worth in. Where we really operate is on the state level, and that goes for First Mutual Trust Company and every large bank in the nation.

Our procedure, I'm sure, is fairly similar to the method used by most banks. Our legal department issues a lengthy document containing a summary of every banking bill being introduced into the state legislature. It is simply a brief breakdown of the dozens of bills which may be proposed in any given year, and wisely, the legal department never suggests which side of a particular legislative fence we might be on. However, it takes only an ability to read while moving your lips to figure out which bills the bank would like passed and which it would like sunk.

Although no memorandum has ever been circulated throughout the bank and although there is absolutely nothing on record, each officer at our bank is expected to go through the list of bills before the legislature. And we are expected to go through the list of legislators to see if there is anyone we know serving as a senator or assemblyman. If we spot a friend, old acquaintance or even the surly neighbor who leaves his garbage cans in the front of the house, we are expected to get in touch with the legislator in question and put in a good word for our side.

Because I live in New Jersey, I am exempted from spending any time going over the bills or making useless telephone calls to high school cronies who have landed on their feet in Albany, New York, and are determining the fate of the state. Nonetheless, I do get the list of bills along with everyone else, and it makes for pleasant weekend reading. One year — the year all of the New York banks dipped their toes into the credit card ocean — a flood of bills involving credit cards was introduced. One law required the credit card issuer (the bank, for example) to send to the credit card holder by registered mail, with a return receipt, a copy of adverse credit information pertaining to the holder, at least one week before the issuer (again the bank) discloses such information to another. That means, among other things, that if you think you're going to stiff us and American Express at the same time, you're wrong. It also means that you, the card holder, don't have much of a chance, because if we find out anything we deem detrimental to your credit rating, we're going to be damned big blabbermouths in a hurry. If, in the northeastern section of the United States, it now takes at least four days and sometimes longer for a letter to travel from Boston to Washington, all the return receipt requesteds in the world aren't going to protect the consumer who just might disagree with that adverse credit information.

One year another bill made it an unlawful discriminatory practice for a banking organization to make a distinction or discrimination in rates, terms, or conditions of mortgage on residential property because of race, religion, color, national origin or ancestry of applicant or owner, mortgagor, lessee, tenant, occupant, or other having interest in realty which is subject to loan. Nonsense.

Immediately following that bill was another which said, in effect, that if we reject your application or credit because of information given to us by a credit bureau, we must disclose to you *upon request* the name and address of the credit bureau, and if you learn that much you'll also learn that you've got the right to write the credit bureau involved and they must give you reasonable opportunity to examine the files. Lots of luck. Nine out of ten people don't know they have the right and we're not going around advertising the fact. You'll also note that, even though you do get your hands on the information, nothing in the bill gives you relief from the information, except now you've got it in hand. Not one word there about appealing the opinion of the credit bureau, is there?

One year the penal code of the State of New York was amended as follows: *to make it misdemeanor for agent, director, officer, or employee of banking association to receive gift, gratuity or thing of value upon understanding that his vote, opinion, judgment, action, decision or other official proceeding shall be influenced thereby, or that he will do any act or neglect official duty in connection with any loan to be made or extended by any banking organization.* Catch the misdemeanor, rather than the felony. Also catch the gaping holes in the amendment, one of which is "thing of value." Someplace along the line, a lobbyist worked very hard to make it a misdemeanor, not a felony.

Still another proposed credit card law had this terrific clause in it: *with unlawful possession of one card to be class A misdemeanor and unlawful possession of two or more cards to be class B felony.* Not a word about seven credit cards. The origin of that bill is crystal clear: just about every bank in New York that issued credit cards botched the job, resulting in thousands of customers possessing many more thousands of credit cards. There was cheering at our bank when that bill was dropped in the hopper.

One of the most controversial amendments to the banking laws was this gem: *interest shall be paid by any bank or trust company on moneys invested in Christmas Clubs, Vacation Plans or similar forms of account at rate determined by banking organization or board of directors, not to ex-*

*ceed maximum rate as defined herein.* We had little at stake in that law because we had decided to pay interest on our Christmas Clubs before it was mandatory. But some banks in New York didn't and must have fought like hell to prevent this bill from going through. It got passed, though, and now all banks — finally — have to pay interest. It was another polite form of ripping off the customer until consumer pressure got too great and the banks had to cave in and give interest.

If you've ever bought a house and wondered if the bank paid your taxes the way they were supposed to, you now can relax at last: *it shall be the duty of such organization to make payments when they become due, and that organization shall be liable to mortgagor for any damages he may sustain due to default.* Small suburban banks, through design or sloppiness, have been known to miss tax payments. When an owner's house suddenly vanished at a sheriff's sale to meet back taxes, the owner had no one to blame but his blameless bank. Now the bank has got to watch its bookkeeping.

Here's a lovely, if innocuous-sounding, bill: *to allow investment in such securities [estates, powers and trusts] as would be acquired by prudent men of discretion and intelligence who are seeking reasonable income and preservation of capital, subject to specifications in written instructions or by court order.* To which I might add: not only must the trust officers be prudent men who are discreet, intelligent, and reasonable, but it also wouldn't hurt if they spoke and dressed well. The heart quavers at the leeway given to trust officers under the provision of that law, and I've yet to come up with a good definition of a prudent man when the stock market goes into a nosedive.

Not all bills are for commercial banks; the savings banks and the savings and loan associations have their friends, too. Viz.: *to allow investments by savings banks in obligations for purchase of railroad rolling stock . . . and to include purchase of aircraft engines, propellers, appliances or spare parts.* The co-sponsors of that bill probably were the Penn Central and Lockheed.

On and on the list goes. Most of the bills quietly slip through the legislature unnoticed and are surely not generally known to the consumer. Many of the bills seem to favor the banks. The consumer has his allies, but somehow they seem to be outnumbered.

Certain members of the legislature seem to be proposing an awful lot of bills on the side of the banks. Far be it from me to name those lawmakers or cite the bills, or even imply the remotest connection between legislator and industry.

I noted with some satisfaction that a particularly nasty bill, aimed directly at the consumer, had been proposed by a gentleman who later was found guilty in New York on totally unrelated charges; he didn't make it to Albany for the next session, but rather to jail. I think the only conclusion that I can draw is that banks have lobbyists, just like other industries, and we seem quite well organized and structured. Left behind in the lurch, as always, is the consumer, and it is a sad commentary on our state legislature that he doesn't seem to have many friends in court, at least when it comes to the banking industry.

# CHAPTER X

A few years ago in one of our all-black branches in Bedford-Stuyvesant in Brooklyn, the following sequence of events took place. An employee of ours who was a teller brought a friend of his into the branch. He introduced the friend, whom I had better call Richard, to one of the platform assistants named Nicholas, and told Nicholas that Richard was a car salesman by profession and an okay guy and please cash his check. Richard the car salesman did not have an account with us; thus, he needed someone on the platform to approve the check.

Richard soon developed an easygoing relationship with Nicholas, our platform assistant. Richard's friend, the teller, quit the bank and moved on to greener pastures, but Richard still came into our bank and by this time was quite close to Nicholas. As I said, the teller who originally introduced Richard to us was black, the platform assistant Nicholas was black, and Richard was black. As are all of the personnel of that branch.

Richard and Nicholas got so chummy that at Christmas Richard came in with a bottle of Scotch and gave it to Nicholas, just as a token of his appreciation for being such a nice person. After about a year of check-cashing, Richard complained one day to Nicholas that he sure didn't like standing around the long lines at the teller windows to cash his checks. Did his friend Nicholas have any suggestions? As a matter of fact, Nicholas did, especially since not one of Richard's checks had bounced. What Nicholas could do would be to walk Richard over to the general cage window, where the larger and more sophisticated transactions took place, and tell the general cage clerk, a man named Adams, that it was okay to cash Richard's check. And so in the second year of the friendship between Nicholas and Richard, Richard had moved up to the general cage and now had a new friend at the bank, Adams. The checks became a mite more frequent, but still not one bit of trouble; no fancy footwork concerning the dating of a check, no whisper of what was about to come.

(Let me interrupt myself for a moment to say that among the three people mentioned so far — Richard, Nicholas, and Adams — no fewer than five explicit rules of First Mutual Trust had been broken at this point and the figure probably was closer to ten. Little things, like the casual cashing of checks without proper identification. But rules and regulations are one thing, and friendship is another.)

To continue the scenario. One day Richard stepped in, beaming over a splendid transaction he'd just made at the car lot, and asked Nicholas to approve a $2,000 check. Of course. Richard went over to the general cage where his good friend Adams cashed the check and must have suffered momentary blindness, because he gave Richard $2,-500 instead of $2,000. This was discovered because at the end of the day Adams was short $500 and couldn't account for it. Whether he realized that the $500 was residing in Richard's jeans or not, I don't know.

A week later, enter Richard, with still another check to

cash. The check was approved without a hitch, and given to Adams to cash. Adams was struck with an inspiration, because as he handed over some fresh money he said to Richard, "Hey, Richard, I didn't happen to give you an extra $500 last week, did I?" Richard allowed as how he did have an extra $500 as a result of the $2,000 check, and as a gesture of good will and bonhomie, he handed back to Adams $210. I don't know where he came up with such a crazy figure, but he did. One week later, Richard walked in and handed over to Adams another $200, and at that Adams thought Richard was the next best thing to the Prince of Peace. If you've been keeping track of this with pencil and paper, the bank is out $90 so far.

Two weeks after Richard had almost squared the books with us, he breezed in with a big check — a *very* big check, some $7,000 worth. As luck would have it, his hard-working pal Nicholas had taken leave of the platform for a well-deserved vacation. But this didn't faze Richard; he simply went over to the general cage and there was Adams, not on vacation, but with plenty of cash on hand. Without a second thought, Adams laid seven big ones on Richard, which in a white, blue, green or chartreuse section of New York is a damned good score. You don't normally skip with $7,000 without some kind of questions.

You needn't be Edgar Cayce to figure out what happened next. The $7,000 check bounced like a rocket, and when the auditors and the regional personnel descended upon the bank, they asked Adams how in God's name he could have cashed such a check without any kind of credentials.

Adams gave what I consider a very logical and sensible answer: "Well, I knew that Nicholas was on vacation, but if he had been here he would have approved it. So I cashed it." And I agree. Richard had gulled everyone for two years, and they probably would have cashed anything under $100,000 without a flicker.

Because this branch is in a black area, and because we are extremely sensitive about the relationships between the bank, our branches, and ghetto neighborhoods, we did not move in on the branch the way we might have in a white neighborhood. We decided to write off the $7,090 (the $90, you will recall, is what was left from the overpayment of $500 some three checks ago) and try to explain to all hands that the bank didn't jive this way. The manager of the branch, a man named Baker; Nicholas, the platform assistant; Adams, the general cage clerk — all shook their heads at the bank's cupidity and went back to work, presumably sadder but wiser. Nobody ever expected to see Richard again.

Imagine the surprise, then, when in walked Richard the following week without a worry bead in sight. He and Nicholas and Baker, the branch manager, immediately pulled up three chairs and had a conference. Richard admitted that the $7,000 check had more latex in it than normal and he said he was going to get out on the car lot and sell like hell to make it back. In the meantime, he said, what he'd like to do would be to open a checking account with $1,-000, which he just happened to have in cash in his pocket.

Whatever was blurring the minds of Nicholas and Adams also struck manager Baker, because he agreed. He later said that he thought it would be more beneficial to have at least $1,000 in the bank than nothing. It did not occur to him to chain Richard to a desk and call the cops. So Richard now had a brand-new checking account with us, $1,-

ooo in the account, and this time he fled the coop for good.

"Fuck this race relations shit," said a security man as he prepared an all-points bulletin on friend Richard. And this time around the auditors, the security people, the regional inspectors — none of them were as nice as they had been when they'd come in the first time. The general cage clerk and the platform assistant were immediately fired.

They promptly said that they were going after Richard with armor and they expected to have the $6,090 back in a short time. They wanted to know if they returned all of the money, could they have their jobs back? We said, "Bring back the money and we'll talk about it, and don't give us any details about the remains of Richard." As for the manager, Baker, everyone held their head and said, "Let's try again."

As things stand now, no one has returned: like the money, Richard, Nicholas, and Adams are apparently gone with the wind.

The real tragedy of this tale is, first, that it's true and second, that Nicholas and Adams probably returned to the jobs they'd held before they entered banking. Nicholas had been a janitor and Adams had been a window washer. They had both gone through one of our myriad job opportunity programs and slowly had risen through the ranks to general cage clerk and platform assistant. Not only had years of hard work gone out the window, but the job opportunity program suffered as well.

The story of Richard and his friends is not unusual and is repeated quite often in every bank engaged in urban programs. The circumstances might change from bank to bank, but tragedies like this are enacted every week of the year. I've told the story because it gives the reader and the nonbanker just a taste of the race relations problems which face banks today. There can be no question that one of the underlying and recurrent failures of banks has been their policies and attitudes involving race.

Most bankers want to walk away from the race problem, but they can't. Most banks are as backward about race relations as any other segment of American industry; in fact, we might be more backward. But the seriousness of the problem is compounded not just because of the blacks we employ, but because of the vast sums of money we control.

Despite the fact that banks in general, and our bank in particular, are equal opportunity employers, most of the blacks in banks are working in the lower-grade clerical areas, in the check-processing division, in any operation which is behind the scenes. Demand deposit accounting — a hidden function in the bank — is black-staffed, as are the operations of the credit card division. But . . . we have only a handful of vice presidents who are black; there aren't any senior or executive vice presidents who are black; and I can guarantee you that the president, the vice chairman and the chairman of the board are whiter than white. The board of directors is all white; and although it may come to pass that a token black — probably an educator — might eventually find his way onto the board, he won't have any influence.

I cannot speak for all banks in New York City, or the United States, or the world, but I can guess that our situation is not unique. I doubt whether many West Indians or Pakistanis hold positions of influence in any of Great Britain's leading banks. Our bank, like all banks, is right there in the forefront of active recruiting for qualified black personnel. We are in touch with all of the right black institutions. In fact, if you want, you can recruit at Atlanta University, Morris Brown College, Morehouse College, Howard University, Hampton Institute, Clark College, and a couple more. In New York City, there are at least two dozen programs or organizations dealing with minorities. These range from the well-known organizations like the Urban League to local groups such as the South Bronx Concentrated Employment Service.

We make all the right moves, say all the right things, join all the right programs, donate to all the right charities, and then a first vice president says casually in passing, "I need a new secretary, but no darkies please." That is the crux of the banking problem. We will approve the contribution and issue the obligatory memo, but don't allow "them" on the executive floor.

I have thought long and hard about banks and race, and the depressing conclusion I have come to is that if contemporary society is indifferent to the plight of the black, then banks aren't even in step with society. We're lagging behind society, when we should at least be in step, no matter how backward society is. Ideally, banks should be trying to lead, be a step in front. In some segments of contemporary society, busing does occur peacefully, integration does work to a certain extent, housing can become mixed without block-busting. But we're not even up to busing at this point.

Yet the directives from the head of our bank point out, in no uncertain terms, that we are to utilize minority group employees through the whole spectrum of jobs and insure them equal consideration whenever promotional opportunities occur. This last sentence, by the way, is almost word for word from one of the memos on the subject. In reality it doesn't happen, and the common complaint heard throughout the bank is, "We just can't find the qualified people." You don't have to go into a bank to hear this, either; it's thrown at you in practically every industry in the country.

As for our seeking qualified people, one of the most powerful black organizations sends us about 250 résumés each year, résumés of people the organization feels are qualified to be hired at a minimum of $10,000 a year. The organization says politely but firmly that we should be hiring at least 100 of these 250 people, and if we don't hire any of the applicants they would like to have the résumé back with a detailed explanation of why the person was not qualified.

One of the many programs we sponsor is actually a part-time school for minorities who need basic educational skills. We put these people on the payroll at $85 a week and send them to school half days five days a week. After many months of intensive education, they graduate and are absorbed into the bank.

Despite our programs, and despite the constant flood of well-meaning memos from the executive suite, I still can't escape the feeling that we are being forced into the programs. We really don't have a social conscience; the various minority organizations are forcing a conscience on us.

Although we don't have any fixed quota of black officers, we are very concerned that promising young blacks and Puerto Ricans have to start rising through the officer ranks as well. How far they rise with us — well, that's a difficult question which no one has the answer to.

Occasionally an officer in a position of responsibility and power does see the problems which are going to hit all banks right in the face. But more often than not, the officer with the authority to alter our attitude grew up in a white suburb, went to a white university, lives in a white suburb not far from where he was raised, and wouldn't know 125th Street from Bedford-Stuyvesant. Here is a portion of a memo written by such an officer: "Our purpose in the urban affairs program is to increase our profits. In the poorer communities of Brooklyn, through a better marketing plan, we recognize the need of a new kind of approach beyond the opportunities provided by our present offices. It emphasizes the broader approach to the influential black market within the area and the expectation that as this market becomes more affluent we will have the groundwork for a better share of the market."

He's talking about the *increasing* affluence of the market. Yet as far as anyone can tell who's ever seen the tragedy of Bedford-Stuyvesant at first hand, many of these people are barely able to eat or find a decent place to live. Nevertheless his memo starts with the proposition that our first object is to increase our profits, and he feels that with our clever marketing we're going to have the bulk of the business as soon as the market gets a little richer.

His attitude is a little more cynical than most, but it certainly is representative. Every other year, a new mortgage program is announced by the bank with a great deal of fanfare, and when it is made public we piously say that it is aimed toward the black. But it's not so new and it isn't aimed at anyone in particular, because we still require 25 percent down on the purchase price of the house; and my feeling is that the ghetto dweller certainly wants to own his own home, but he doesn't have anywhere near the 25 percent down payment required. Again and again we talk big and then produce very little.

We're no better than any other bank when it comes to writing off the ghetto population. Sherman J. Maisel, a member of the Federal Reserve Board, warned banks back in 1971 to stop making loans only to the affluent suburbs while neglecting the inner city. He said that banks have found it extremely profitable "to concentrate their loans in new homogeneous suburbs while red-lining major sectors of the inner city. . . . [This policy] helped create major social and economic problems of crime, decay and segregation." He said that such lending policies "may insure short-run profitability at the costly premium of foregone long-run profitability." That's a very good and strong point of view, except that he made it to a meeting of the National Conference of Christians and Jews, an organization one would hope would agree with him. What the bankers think of such a policy is a different matter.

Occasionally, banks mix oranges and apples. A couple of years ago every person in the bank got an IBM card with a checklist to be filled out. The bank wanted to know if you were black, Spanish-speaking, Indian, Chinese (but not Japanese), Jewish, or, in the words of that great egalitarian, "other." All of this data was collated in personnel so the bank would know at a glance how much of our staff was black, Chinese, or "other." And if any pressure group came at us with a demand that we weren't hiring enough Indians, we were able to produce instantly the proof that we did have a few Indians whooping it up and that our percentage of Indians was consistent with the proportion of Indians to the general population. The fallacy, obviously, is that we can say that we have so many black officers, but we are not breaking down the mass of statistics to show whether the black officers are truly influential in the bank's policies.

On the working level, the stresses are apparent daily. A customer walked into one of our branches seeking a loan, and the loan representative, a woman, turned the man's application down without a valid explanation. The man, a black, said that he was going to report the incident to the NAACP. The woman, a tough cookie from Staten Island, said, "Listen, buddy, I got a guy in Brooklyn who will kill you for $50 if you give me any trouble."

As more blacks are given jobs of responsibility which bring them into direct contact with the public, attitudes of the public are also going to change. I doubt whether many banks in this country have black trust officers handling white customers' accounts. Most black officers are hidden — literally speaking — from public view. Eventually, black officers are going to graduate from the operations level and reach the customer level. When we arrive at this point, any preconceived notions customers might have about blacks will have to vanish too.

Three years ago, the National Educational Television network put on a one-hour documentary entitled "Banks and the Poor," which was a revealing and graphic look at the way banks operate. On the side of the banks were David Rockefeller of Chase Manhattan and a man named Nat Rogers, president of the American Banking Association. On the side of the consumer were Representative Wright Patman, an attorney, and Bess Myerson, who at the time was the commissioner of the New York City Department of Consumer Affairs.

In a memorandum circulated to all of us (and I assume to every bank in the country), First Mutual Trust admitted that the picture painted by the television program was not overly friendly, but perhaps we ought to take a look in case we had to debate angry consumers or customers. After watching the program I figured it at Critics 3, Banks zip. Patman and his friends took the banks and the bankers over the coals, and they had the documentation to do it. Under discussion was a $100 million mortgage lending pool, put together by 80 banks to rehabilitate Bedford-Stuyvesant. The former chairman of Chase Manhattan, George Champion, was quoted as saying, "We are involved because it is the right, the humanitarian, the moral, the Christian-like thing to do."

Attorney James Finney, a NAACP lawyer, said that while the pool was created in 1968, in the two succeeding years only $8 million had been lent out (the program was aired on November 9, 1970). Finney charged Chase with making available only $700,000, and he added that the pool was restricted to houses of four families or less, which "won't affect 80 percent of the families in Bedford-Stuyvesant." Chase's Rockefeller replied, "I'm bound to say that like some other projects with high ideals and objectives, it was a little slow in getting off the ground. . . . We're committed to invest up to $5 million. . . . We have, however, through our real estate and mortgage department, given a good deal of assistance to the program and we're hopeful that it is going to move faster in the future. We're eager to put the money out if the opportunities present themselves." To which Patman retorted: "In the Chase Manhattan Bank, as big as it is, worth fifteen or twenty billion dollars, they were putting a few million dollars in housing, just a very few, a very insignificant amount. . . ." Patman ended his attack by saying, "They have had plenty of money for everything, except one of the essentials of family life — adequate housing. They didn't have any money for that."

Patman and Rockefeller spent a lot of useless time arguing about Patman's well-known hostility toward banks. Rockefeller, repeating the apocryphal story, said: "Congressman Patman is a very distinguished and successful politician. I think his prejudices and biases in the banking industry are quite well known. I understand that he was once turned down for some loan that he tried to make in his local Texas bank, and he seems to have taken a rather dim view of bankers ever since." Patman later replied, "The fiction about Wright Patman isn't the issue. The issue is what the big banks are doing against low-income Americans."

Rockefeller pointed out that Chase had, at the time of the broadcast, some $3 billion in mortgage and real estate loans, to which Patman said, "He talks about real estate loans, but he is really talking about massive investments in office buildings and in luxury housing, not the kind of housing that is really needed."

At the time the program was made, it was calculated that savings and loan associations controlled assets of $169,630,000,000; today that figure is above $206,-000,000,000. The program charged that although savings and loan associations are chartered to finance housing, less than 1 percent of their assets were diverted to low-income housing. Additionally, savings and loan associations were accused of fostering slum housing by financing absentee landlords. All of which was roundly denied by representatives of such savings institutions. The producers of the program dug up the story of a two-block-long Washington, D.C., slum, financed by a $132,750 loan from the Jefferson Federal Savings & Loan Association made to a real estate company, which just happened to be headed by a landlord who was a director of Jefferson Federal. And if you needed further proof of interlocking directorships, the president of Jefferson Federal turned out to be a vice president of the real estate company involved.

As I've said, the program was produced three years ago. But despite David Rockefeller's eloquent defense of Chase's role in revitalizing deteriorating neighborhoods, all one has to do is walk (with heart in hand) through the devastated sections of Brooklyn. They resemble Dresden in 1945 more than the United States of America today. Patman's point that Chase's allocation of a top of $5 million to Bedford-Stuyvesant is but a drop in Chase's bucket is terribly valid.

The point that neither adversary on the program got into was the headache any chief executive officer of any public corporation faces. The officer, and let us use Rockefeller as an example, is answerable to his Board of Directors and his shareholders. The bank is under a myriad of regulations — local, state, and federal — all outlining the specific obligations of a chartered bank. Rockefeller simply cannot say, "Let's change mortgage requirements for Brooklyn residents." The public David Rockefeller is not a charitable organization: he has an obligation, like all business organizations, to show a profit on capital invested. But the private David Rockefeller, as a very rich individual, is an entirely different story. He could, if he wished, donate $10 million to the residents of Brooklyn and let them do what they wanted to with the money.

If Chase were to drastically revise their mortgage policy and announce bravely that henceforth 90 percent of the funds allocated to mortgages were going to be funneled to the urban ghetto, Chase the bank and public corporation would be in a peck of trouble. The little old ladies padding through their golden years on Chase dividends would raise the very dickens with Rockefeller.

Our chairman at First Mutual Trust issues a staggering number of well-meaning memoranda from his office on the subject of being nice to your fellow man. And he believes it, too. What our chairman hasn't done is to take a large chunk of our capital and say, specifically, "Take this money and go into the ghettos with it and do some good." He's Mr. Nice Guy, but there are limits to these things.

I don't know whether Patman really understands this problem with the banks. He can summon them before any committee he wants to and every chief executive officer of every bank in the country is going to say to him that banks honestly want to help the urban ghettos. But can they really deliver? Do all of their officers on their staffs believe the liberal rhetoric?

When Rockefeller recently fired the president of Chase he didn't give a specific reason for the change, but everyone in banking knew that Chase had relinquished its number one position in New York City to First National City; and Chase's former global superiority had been chipped away by Manufacturers Hanover of New York as well as by First National City. That's not ego-tripping on the part of Chase: it's plain and simple earnings per share and Rockefeller didn't have Bedford-Stuyvesant on his mind when he made the change.

Banks react; they don't act. When the ghettos blow up in the surprised faces of the savings and loan institutions and banks, then the banks will realize that they do indeed have a responsibility which directly affects their pocketbooks. As long as banks are kept within certain geographic limitations, then they literally cannot escape the central city. Today the cities are functioning enough for the banks to function. If the central cities fail to function because of racial warfare, thus making the banking business an anachronism, then the banks will act.

The response inside banks, and the ruling structure of banks, will probably come about the same way. When an organization — in terms of sheer numbers — has a minority as half of its work force, then the organization must respond. And banks won't be able to hide their black officers the way they do now. Black personnel officers obviously are in vogue as the clerical and operations staffs become more black-dominated. This pressure from underneath will force and is forcing banks to place more black officers in positions of responsibility.

Will a black ever become the president of a major bank anywhere? My guess is yes, in another twenty years or so. The thing the banks can't evade is that blacks are slowly, painfully, but steadily becoming truly integrated into white society. When banks wake up to this, a black will become president of a bank. Right now, a few banks across the country are finally letting a black or two onto their boards of directors. This trend will increase. There are very few blacks currently on the boards of New York banks, but I feel this exclusion will change quite soon. Banks aren't private clubs any more; they want black, as well as white, deposits; and more than ever they depend on black labor to keep them functioning.

Labor conditions for all bank employees are horrible, be they black or white. The salary scales for clerks, tellers, and "those people" (as officers refer to them) are abysmally low.

When the cops arrived to put the collar on Roswell Steffen, the man who supervised all the tellers at a branch of the Union Dime Savings Bank, the officers at the bank were staggered. Here was their forty-one-year-old employee — and just a chief teller, not an officer — who they thought was sublimely happy earning $11,000 a year, and living in a two-bedroom garden apartment in New Jersey with his wife and two daughters. The take-home pay on $11,000 a year can't be more than $8,500, or somewhere in the neighborhood of $163 a week. Perhaps he took home $9,000 a year, or something like $170 a week. No matter how you look at it, he wasn't well paid for the position he held and the responsibility he had. Serious financial difficulties are bad enough. Being a compulsive gambler on top of that might well have been fatal in his case.

The banking officials quoted by the *Times* said that computer manipulations are on the rise, and more and more cases of embezzlement are taking place nowadays with the aid of computers. As I said at the beginning of this book, had not the cops discovered that the teller in this case was an enormous bettor, God knows how long it would have taken the bank to uncover the fact. If I were the president of Union Dime (who quickly pointed out that the bank was fully covered by insurance), I would have to wonder something about the computer systems, the people who had access to the systems, and how much I paid the people who had the access.

(I ought to point out that while salaries differ slightly from coast to coast, all of the salaries quoted in this book are quite accurate, even in a geographical sense. Although it is true that the starvation wages paid to tellers in banks may have risen $5 or $10 a week since the book was begun in 1971, it is correspondingly true that wage freezes and inflation have wiped out even the small gains that low-ranking personnel have made.)

Banks have long operated under a two-class system: officers and others. Officers had all the incentive in the world: profit-sharing, stock options, better conditions. The only incentive in the world for a nonofficer was to play with the system, become a teller, hope to reach the position of chief teller. Roswell Steffen had become a chief teller, but somewhere along the line he seems to have found the chief teller's life wanting.

The real problem in controlling the profit and loss in a bank is that a bank is not selling automobiles, and if the cost of material and labor is rising in an inflationary market, the bank cannot casually add on $100 to the sticker price. Banks don't have anything to sell but money, and the price that banks can charge for money is not a competitive variable. Prime rates for one are prime rates for all: Chase can't charge 7½ percent to its good customers, with First National City sneaking in at 6½ percent. The Federal Reserve Board does not like that kind of behavior.

A bank consists of real estate, money which brings in revenue, and people. People — payroll — is the real swing variable in profit and loss. When First Mutual Trust held its massacre, we saved millions. The controllable factor in a bank's profits is salary administration. It is no mystery to bankers that banks have traditionally not paid their people well. Banks, unlike corporations which dealt in *things,* knew and know that the one dependable control they do have is salary, and traditionally the salaries have been as low as possible.

Banks managed to get by on low salaries by holding out

the promise of opportunity to their people: stick with us and if you're good, someday you'll grow up and become an officer. But once the ambition leaves the working class and they come to realize that truly there is a two-class system, then there is going to be hell to pay.

If the day ever arrives where the AFL-CIO decides that perhaps it's time to organize bank workers, banks are going to have to revolutionize their thinking in a hurry. Up till now, banks have got by on the absolute blind and dumb devotion to them by their workers. But this devotion has steadily been eroding in the past five years or so. A new breed of bank worker has come into the bank: the worker who doesn't give a damn about the bank, who realizes immediately that there is really very little opportunity for him, and who understands that devotion is not going to get him anything if money is tight and the bank has to let go 10 percent of its clerical staff. And the work force today is more sophisticated and less bound by typical middle-class morality. If you went into the operating sector of any bank and guaranteed a couple of the computer people that you had a surefire scheme for stealing from the bank, they'd shake hands without hesitation. Twenty years ago, your offer would have been reported immediately. But twenty years ago we weren't run by faceless computers, today we are. And if a clerk can figure out how to extract money from any old IBM 360, he's not going to lie awake at nights worrying about his discoveries.

The idea of the work force of a bank going out on strike is the kind of thought that has never occurred to a banker, because it represents the impossible. But if police, or firemen, or city workers, or hospital technicians are able to bring their respective institutions to a halt, who is to say that the bank workers of America can't unite for better salaries, better benefits, a larger share of the pie? Work forces with little attachment to the institution that employs them are those work forces ripest for organized labor. When banks truly were family affairs, and the president looked after his people and knew practically every employee by name, no union would have dared to try and organize a bank. But banks have been conglomerating (if that is the correct terminology) and the management is much more remote than it has ever been. Branches proliferate, computers abound, and the bank president as stern but fair father figure doesn't exist anymore. Nobody I know regards David Rockefeller as a father figure, with the exception of his children — and I really can't speak for them. And David Rockefeller is just as likely to be popping in and out of Romania as he is to be showing up to congratulate the branch at Third Avenue and Forty-sixth Street in New York City.

Although the black worker in a bank is ambitious and truly wants to get ahead, he knows better than anyone else that the bank really doesn't care about him. Because if the black has been raised in Harlem, or the South or East Bronx, or anywhere where the banks aren't, he really has a bead on the bank's true motives. The black bank worker might well be more ripe for organizing than the white, but the white's understanding of his status vis-à-vis the bank is getting more sophisticated every day and pretty soon he will have caught up to the black in his insight.

But these are minor considerations in the scheme of the future. What worries me most is housing and the central city. Banks and savings and loan institutions are more than willing to lend you money up to Ninety-sixth Street in New York City, but they draw the line at Ninety-seventh. Obvious faults in mortgage lending can and should be controlled by state legislatures. The cross-fertilization so apparent in the previously cited Jefferson Savings & Loan deal in Washington, D.C., can be fixed. What is infinitely more difficult to straighten out is nonactivity. Can a government force a private lending institution to finance housing — either single or multiple dwelling — which the private institution says is not profitable? The banker cries socialism.

The only massive attempt at inner-city renewal today comes through taxes and through the government and various Federal Housing Agency programs. Nothing very substantive or noteworthy is being done in the private sector. And the Nixon Administration these days is certainly not showing any inclination toward increasing government aid to the inner cities; indeed, most of the government's response to the pleas of city and state governments has been to cut back or eliminate federally supported programs, whether in education, or day care, or housing.

I don't know what the answer is, but I do know the critical point is rapidly approaching. I cannot conceive that any bank, in New York, Chicago, London or anywhere, which derives its income from the business activity of the central city will allow the central cities to vanish in a puff of smoke. That a revolution has to be forthcoming in bank management and mentality is inevitable.

In terms of revolution, the women's fight for equal rights ranks right about where the blacks do in banks. We have a handful of women officers, and although they aren't openly discriminated against (here again, this is against a mass of city, state, and federal laws), the prejudice remains nonetheless.

We do have a few women officers at First Mutual Trust.

To talk about them in specific terms would, since we have so few, both identify them and First Mutual Trust. Granted, women have begun to make progress in the last couple of years. Women are beginning to be allowed to manage branches — all by themselves. And the few women officers we have are finally being allowed to break out of the traditional slots for women in banks: public relations and personnel.

The situation with women parallels the black crisis almost point for point. Most of our tellers are women; many of our back office personnel are women; and although we don't know how many of our deposits are controlled by women, if bank deposits are anything comparable to national statistics, then women have one hell of a lot of money in our bank. To date, the women in banks have yet to show as much militancy as the blacks in terms of seeking more power and equal status for themselves. Yet inevitably, women who are seeking a career in banks are going to make their presence felt. When the women start pressuring for change in banks right along with blacks, many of the sacred and hoary traditions are going to tumble. This can't happen soon enough for me.

# CHAPTER XI

A couple of days ago a friend of mine called to say he was going to turn over all his financial affairs to his bank and let them do his estate planning. This fellow used to let his bills pile up in an elegant silver bowl. Every six months, when the bills flowed over the sides of the silver bowl, he would sit down and pay them in a grand orgy of check writing. When he asked me what I thought of having a bank do his estate planning, I had to honestly say that they certainly couldn't do any worse than he'd been doing, and they might be able to improve on things.

Which brings us to the final question of what should you trust banks with and what uses should you make of banks. Many years ago, when I first started working for First Mutual Trust, I was put into the trust department for a couple of years and allowed to manage a few portfolios. I learned then that banks managing money are just as human as anyone else managing money: everyone is a hero when the stock market is flying and we're all bums when the market is going down ten points a day. Banks get the same kind of panic telephone calls that stockbrokers do when the market collapses.

The first thing I learned as a junior trust officer is that very few trust officers in very few banks anywhere in the world really have anything to say about the management of the portfolios they are handling. Once a month — at least this is the way it used to be in the trust department — a handy confidential report would come around to all of us. Although the report was only fifteen pages long, it was brilliantly designed and laid out so that it covered the bank's recommendations on just about 450 different stocks, which were mostly companies listed on the New York Stock Exchange or the American Stock Exchange. Aside from an up-to-date digest of yearly price range, dividend information, price/earnings ratio, and estimated earnings, the report also had a clever formula whereby the dumbest trust officer could glance at a stock and instantly tell a customer whether to hold, sell, or buy more.

The bank ranked stocks from 1 to 4, which indicated the degree of risk inherent in the stock generally. 1, naturally, was the best, 4 the worst; and it was left up to the individual trust officer to figure out the permutations between 2 and 3. But after each number was a letter code as well: A meant buy; B was for hold; C told the trust officer to sell if he wished; and D was the warning to pull out instantly, the auditors were at work. 1A thus ranked at the top and 4D the bottom. All of this information was generated by the investment research division of the bank, and throughout the years they proved to be terribly cautious, but in the long haul terribly correct, about the stock market. As long ago as 1969 and 1970, the bank was recommending other bank stocks and looking askance at the shenanigans of conglomerates, high flyers, and electronics companies run out of garages.

The problem in dealing with a bank's recommendations is that in a hot market the customer is eager to buy stocks

that are covered once a week in the over-the-counter listings, and the bank is hardly aware that such a thing as the
over-the-counter market exists. I exaggerate, but only
slightly. Nevertheless, if you were to ask me whether to follow the recommendations of a bank's trust department
rather than a brokerage house, there's no doubt in my mind
at all. Take the bank every time.

Despite the conservatism of banks and their investments,
some trust situations do come apart at the seams, and then
you read where a labor pension fund is suing a bank because they're unhappy with the results of their portfolio.
(Forget, for the moment, that the pension fund is liable to
have been riddled with corruption and stupidity of its own.)
The point to remember is that the American economy is
shot to hell today, the American dollar is shot even more to
hell, and although the stock market is still in existence, the
risks of buying common stocks in 1973 are such that a
clairvoyant could do just as well as a stockbroker or a trust
officer.

(In the March 1973 issue of *Esquire,* a writer named
Max Gunther tracked down a fascinating bag of seers, star
gazers, clairvoyants, and even a coven of witches, all of
whom had had a remarkable fling playing the market. They
had done better, on the whole, than most brokerage houses
— and who is to deny what effect the stars have on American Telephone?)

If you are a millionaire, then you know what to do with
your money. If you've got a few thousand dollars in savings, you could take the money to Switzerland, exchange it
for Swiss francs, and let it sit in a Swiss bank. But because
not everyone likes to travel, the alternative is to have your
savings in a savings bank in the United States.

This is not a how-to book, nor was it ever conceived in that fashion. But what follows are my own thoughts on managing money and how much or how little I let my own bank fool with it. Take the thoughts with a grain of salt, and remember that I am writing as an insider, not an outsider.

1. If you don't have a million dollars but you do have a sizable bundle you're not sure what to do with, my inclination would be to avoid letting the bank manage your money for you. A good lawyer is just as able as a bank, and an accountant can advise you what proportion of your money should be in tax-free municipal bonds, savings, common stocks, and real estate. One of the safest things these days are municipal bonds, but bonds, like everything else, can go down in value. What, for example, do you think the worth of Newark municipal bonds are as compared to fifteen years ago? The best investment today probably is real estate, which is why banks are gearing up their real estate investment sections.

2. If you have damned little money, put it into a savings bank and leave it alone. Don't use the savings department of a full service (i.e., commercial) bank unless you have a very good reason to. (About the only valid reason I can think of is if you're having an affair with the savings account teller.) You're losing at least a half a point of interest by not keeping your money in a savings bank, which is strictly for savings, and if you're worried about banks going under, when one type of bank goes, they all go — it doesn't matter what kind they are.

3. When it comes to buying a house, you're going to get screwed — and there is no other way to put it — no matter

where you go for your mortgage. So, with that warming thought in mind, you might as well get your mortgage where your house is. To wit: if you work and bank in Chicago, but want to buy a house in Skokie, Illinois, try for a local savings bank in Skokie rather than your Chicago commercial bank or its branch in Skokie.

4. The best policy is not always the longest or largest mortgage. Sometimes a ten-year mortgage makes more sense than a thirty-year mortgage, no matter how enticing the low down payment seems. If you've got the cash on hand, it sometimes makes sense to pay off your mortgage after the seventh year (if a twenty-year mortgage), depending on what your income is. The point is that you will have taken all the tax benefits at the beginning of the mortgage. (We get our interest first, then the principal.)

5. Don't ever let a bank sucker you into having a regular checking account, or any account called "executive," "first class," or any other madeup name. All such accounts lure you with the promise of no charge for checks you have written, the only hitch is you've got to maintain a minimum balance. Here's the way it works. Depending on where you bank, you'll be charged ten or fifteen cents a check with a special checking account plus a monthly service charge. Even if you write thirty checks a month — and very few people do — that's still no more than $3 or $4.50 a month for the checks plus perhaps another dollar for service. However, if you have to maintain a $500 balance, you are purely and simply giving us $500 to play around with, and let me assure you, we come out ahead on the deal. You're better off keeping the $500 in a savings bank earning something, rather than nothing. It costs us about six cents to process a check and we have to pay that six cents on any

type of account. If you maintain a special checking account, leave as little money as possible in it, keep an accurate checkbook, and calculate your balance down to the last penny.

Let us say that you occasionally have to write a check under harried circumstances (while standing at the cashier's window in Las Vegas). Get traveler's checks. But don't let anyone talk you into a regular checking account because you get a nice laminated card which will "allow you to cash a check at our more than 150 branches in the metropolitan area." Nonsense. If you try to remember where you cash most of your checks, you'll suddenly find you cash 95 percent of them at the same branch of your bank week after week.

6. Don't ever let a bank talk you into one of their fancy "advance checking" propositions. The commercials on these schemes spiel cheerfully of being able to write a check when your balance doesn't have enough to cover the check. I just don't have the energy to point out all the fallacies in these ads, but take my word, there are very few consumer items that can't be held with a deposit.

7. Safe deposit boxes are pretty sensible and you ought to have one.

8. Don't borrow money from a bank to buy a new car, new boat, new television set, new furniture, new clothes, new anything. Show me a man who will borrow money from a bank to take a vacation and I will show you an utter fool.

9. If you are going to establish a relationship with a bank, it does make sense to take out a small bank loan simply to establish credit, and then pay the thing back before it is due. This will cost you a little money (I am assuming you

will immediately take the proceeds of the loan and put it into your savings bank), but it will clear you immediately through the credit system of your bank and will establish you if you ever really need to borrow money.

10. It would be wise to establish a relationship with someone on the platform, remain friendly with them, and say hello now and then. When you have a sticky problem, that platform assistant will come in handy.

11. Don't fool with any bank credit card. It's usually good only in a local context. An American Express card can do as much or more for you than any bank credit card.

12. If you live in a large city in the United States, you are undoubtedly aware that the current trend is toward buying your own condominium or cooperative apartments. Despite what your local bank might be saying in its brochures, and despite what the various state legislatures are passing, you will not find it particularly easy to finance an apartment through your bank. Your savings bank might be a better bet.

13. If you don't have preprinted deposit slips, make sure that when you use one of the bank's deposit slips you carefully check all three copies to make sure someone hasn't put his account number and name on the carbons, leaving you holding the bag with the top copy.

14. Count your money right at the teller's window after a transaction. It saves much wear and tear on the psyche when you find the teller can't count.

15. In case of robbery, fall to the floor and pray like hell.

These are simply a few ideas to keep in mind when dealing with any bank. They do not represent cynicism on my part, only realism. The thrust of this chapter has been to remind you that you really don't have a friend at Chase Manhattan. In fact, you don't have a friend at any bank anywhere at any time. Anybody who thinks that his bank is a chum who really wants to help him struggle through life is mad and ought to be committed.

When you deal with a bank, try to regard that bank as you would anyone you would be doing business with. Banks are not out to cheat you, but they certainly aren't going to give you the house advantage either. If you own a $50 million corporation, they're going to be awfully friendly with you. But if you own a $50 bank balance, don't expect much, even though it is your $50 balance, multiplied by thousands of other $50 balances, which enables them to be friendly with the Widget Hamper System of New Brunswick.

It must be clear by now that I have what could be called mixed feelings about our banks. The question naturally arises, then why do I stay in banking? The answer, which applies to thousands of bankers throughout the world is lethargy. As I have remarked earlier, the life of a vice president in a bank is one of comfort and ease. We really don't work too hard, and once you have reached that comfortable plateau of vice presidency, the tendency is to forget those youthful dreams of glory and start worrying about your nine iron and your forthcoming winter vacation.

I am on the bleak side of forty. Needless to say, if I had known then during those callow days in England, when I first joined the bank, what I know now, I probably would have opted for something else. But I didn't. And when you are contemplating your mortgage, and your forthcoming college loans for children, and your second car, the inspiration to leave the wonderful womb of banking is usually not around. I stay because I stay and I am not unlike my fellow middle-class, middle-rank bank officers. We mark time handsomely, and after we have been in the banking world for fifteen or twenty years, we also mark time cynically.

One of the growing headaches with banks is the image they project. Fifty years ago, banks didn't give a damn about their image, and even twenty years ago, aggressive bank advertising was relatively unknown. But as the importance of retail business grew, advertising and image-making grew as well. Banks like to project themselves as skillfully as Walter Cronkite projects himself: kindly, honest, mature, and one who wouldn't steer you wrong.

Not so. Banks will steer you wrong within the limits of the law if they think they can make an honest buck at it. They send platoons of lobbyists forth daily to make sure that all of the bucks they make are honest, as interpreted by the law.

There is no way to avoid dealing with banks unless you're one of those crazies who can be seen at the post office buying money orders for $10 utility bills. At least deal with banks with your eyes open. The so-called full service bank commercials which flood the airwaves would give you the impression that banks are out there rescuing dying towns, saving floundering industries, helping struggling companies. Well, more towns die than live, more industries collapse than survive, and an awful lot of companies go under for want of a good bank.

I don't think I would go so far as to say that banks are a necessary evil, but I sure do wish they would straighten up and fly right in many areas. Because so many of us depend indirectly on what banks do, they are indeed a public trust.

And that trust is abused too much of the time. If I said that banks needed more federal control I would be burned in the worn-out money incinerator as an heretic. On the other hand, it saddens me that the only national spokesman for the banking consumer is Representative Wright Patman. All of us owe him a debt of gratitude, and I only wish there were 500 Wright Patmans rather than one.

The next time your banker tries to sell you something — from a loan to a tangerine checkbook — look your friendly banker straight in the eye and plumb for truth. Don't ever let your daughter marry a banker, and encourage your son to become a hairdresser before becoming a banker.

And, finally, if you ever have to have any dealings with a finance company, may God have mercy on your soul.

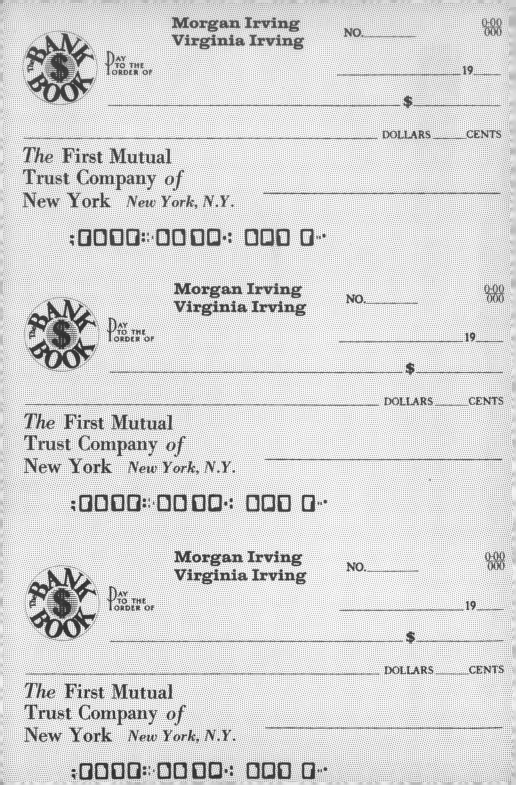

**Morgan Irving**
**Virginia Irving**

NO.

0-00
000

PAY
TO THE
ORDER OF

19

$

DOLLARS \_\_\_\_\_ CENTS

*The* First Mutual
Trust Company *of*
New York  *New York, N.Y.*

;0000: 00 00: 000 0"

**Morgan Irving**
**Virginia Irving**

NO.

0-00
000

PAY
TO THE
ORDER OF

19

$

DOLLARS \_\_\_\_\_ CENTS

*The* First Mutual
Trust Company *of*
New York  *New York, N.Y.*

;0000: 00 00: 000 0"

**Morgan Irving**
**Virginia Irving**

NO.

0-00
000

PAY
TO THE
ORDER OF

19

$

DOLLARS \_\_\_\_\_ CENTS

*The* First Mutual
Trust Company *of*
New York  *New York, N.Y.*

;0000: 00 00: 000 0"